I0008116

Metaverse

An Easy Step-by-step Guide on Discovering

(Digital Asset on the Metaverse and Make Money With Investing)

Archie Andrews

Published By **Andrew Zen**

Archie Andrews

Metaverse: An Easy Step-by-step Guide on Discovering (Digital Asset on the Metaverse and Make Money With Investing)

ISBN   978-1-77485-503-4

Legal & Disclaimer

costs, and expenses, including any legal fees potentially resulting from the application of any of the information provided by this guide. This disclaimer applies to any damages or injury caused by the use and application, whether directly or indirectly, of any advice or information presented, whether for breach of contract, tort, negligence, personal injury, criminal intent, or under any other cause of action.

You agree to accept all risks of using the information presented inside this book. You need to consult a professional medical practitioner in order to ensure you are both able and healthy enough to participate in this program.

TABLE OF CONTENTS

Introduction

The Metaverse is real, and it is going to generate parallel economies that you have to get involved in. Let's talk about the metaverse that falls under thematic type of investing, such as the genomic revolution, next generation Internet, and robotics.

Imagine walking down the street when you consider an item you'd like. Right there is a virtual vending device that is filled with the product as well as all the various variants you've been thinking of. You stop and pick up something in the device, then then it's delivered to your residence. You're interacting with the real world but as well in the virtual world.

Imagine a husband and an wife. The husband is at the shop and the wife is unable to think of the item she requires. The brain-computer interface device in her brain recognizes it and sends the link to her husband's device in the list of stores.

Metaverse is an alternative digital reality in which people can play, work and socialize. It is

1

sometimes referred to as the mirror world or The AR cloud, magical verse, the spatial web and even live maps. It is comprised of 5G machines learning, artificial intelligence as well as edge computing. It's basically a bunch of things gathered together. On a larger scale the Metaverse isn't fully formed yet however, the components are in the process of being constructed and the whole system isn't yet connected. The various technologies must be able to cooperate for this to take place and this will take time.

In relation to Facebook you might have been informed about the fact that Facebook has changed their name from meta to. As per Mark Zuckerberg, they rebranded to be more in line with their new vision of developing technology that allows you to appear as if you were in a virtual reality or even appear in real-world spaces in holograms anywhere in the world.

According to the New York Times, Facebook already has more than 10,000 people working in its labs that are working in Augmented and Virtual reality projects to size. This is roughly double the number of employees for Twitter's entire workforce and, by 2021 Facebook has already spent around 10 billion dollars on metaverse-related investments.

There are many various opportunities and events in the metaverse. You can attend the concert, host meetings and engage in games with your friends and a myriad of other things, and it's almost a virtual place that allows you to build everything.

Chapter 1: The Future Of Finance

Cryptocurrency, non-fungible currency blockchain, augmented reality... The list goes on and on. There's numerous confusing terms that it's difficult to determine where to start. This article will cover all you must be aware of about cryptocurrency, such as how it came into existence and where it's going to go in the near future. We will provide you with a thorough understanding of the essence of cryptocurrency as well as all of its advantages and disadvantages.

Cryptocurrency

In its most basic definition, is a digital representation of money. It can be difficult to comprehend initially, particularly when the habit of having physical copies of bills or coin. In this instance there's no physical piece of metal or leaflet.

What's the problem? Doesn't everything appear a maybe fake? If you don't even be able to see it, and you are unable to even touch it, what can you tell if that it's there? In order to answer that question, we have to revisit the past to think about what "money" even means.

A Short History of Money

Before printing money or coins were made the human race employed a bartering system to exchange and purchase items. Most historians agree that this that it was the most likely arrangement to have taken the past 3,000 years however, there is no definitive evidence of the system, which makes it impossible to trace. The problem in the system was that trades were impeded because of the personal preferences of the participants The person who is #1 may desire what the other person is looking for, but person #2 might not want to trade the item that person #1 has. It was likely that this first led humanity to the notion of using certain items that had an universal value to trade. The first instances of these currencies were animal skins, weapons and salts (Beattie 2021).

Through the ages it was evident that the trend shifted to the usage of gold or silver as a currency, because these commodities also had a high rarity them, which gave them the has the same value that animal pelts had once. This notion of value perception continues to be observed throughout the past, and there was a time when the fourth century B.C. when black pepper, also known as"the King" of Spices was just as precious as gold and could be utilized as a currency, since it was just discovered by Western Europe in the conquests of Alexander the Great. All this, to point out that money as a whole is of no worth other than the value society puts on it.

Then, in the end, humanity witnessed the transition from what is of universal value to what the government considered to be valuable. The centralization of currencies to banks this way and tangible copies of the coins, or eventually paper bills, became more of a receipt than anything else and proved that they had value. The real value was more of an idea than anything else.

But, there are certain issues, even within this system of monetary exchange. It is relatively easy for criminals find and steal information from an account at a bank in the modern world and then to transfer whatever amount of money they'd like. The physical copies of money, too can be passed through without the use of credit or debit cards in general, are, naturally inaccessible, which is why fraudsters make a bigger profit from this.

The idea of cryptocurrency was first conceived in the 1980s, however the first digital currency appeared around 1995. Digicash created from David Chaum. It wasn't a huge success, in a similar way to other attempts like Bitgold. The two initial cryptocurrency had one feature in common: were both heavily encrypted to provide the best protection between a recipient and the donor to make sure that no illicit transactions were happening. This was the first concept of cryptography. It is the process and study of encrypting data so that only the individuals for whom it was intended have access to it.

Bitcoin (BTC) is the very first cryptocurrency that was truly popular created during 2009 by an unidentified person or group under the pseudonym Satoshi Nakamoto. With Nakamoto the problem of a centralised system that could easily be hacked and altered, was resolved. This solution was developed on the basis of a decentralizedpeer-to peer (P2P) network, utilizing blockchain technology.

Beginning at a price of 0.09 USD equals 1 BTC It climbed to an all-time high of 549.14 USD = 1. BTC on November 20, 2021 (Edwards 2021) however, the market remains and will remain unstable due to the constant fluctuations.

The workings inside the Blockchain

Every transaction made on the cryptocurrency platform is recorded in a database known as the ledger. It is an electronic record. Each transaction recorded on the ledger is associated with an individual donor, a person who is the recipient as well as how much money that was exchanged. The recipient and the donor are encoded as highly secure codes.

Since the ledger records every cryptocurrency transaction, the file quickly gets larger in size. Here is the idea of blockchain is introduced. Blockchain is a method for organizing the ledger into blocks and making the information more accessible and simpler for computers to process.

The most significant benefit of cryptocurrency is the decentralization that it achieves by the P2P platform. It is only one Blockchain since it is the only account of all transactions made by the particular currency, yet there are hundreds of thousands of duplicates of the blockchain. The way that the P2P network operates is that users are able to "mine Bitcoin" or mine any other cryptocurrency by renting computers specifically to store and keep a backup replica of the Blockchain. For the exchange of their bitcoin, users will receive an amount of cryptocurrency. This results in hundreds of thousands of computers, all individually updating the ledgers, and therefore there is not one central source of all transactions, rather making them transparent--although encrypted--to everyone. This is because when one version of the ledger differs from all the others, then it's a sign that the culprit has been caught in the act and could be corrected, improving the security of the system.

Different Currencies

To better understand of how cryptocurrency work take a look at Canada as well as its Canadian dollar, also known as CAD. On the other hand, throughout the globe, Japan uses the Japanese yen or JPY. Both currencies, in essence, but they have different value in monetary terms in these various nations. Similar to cryptocurrencies, they are the same as JPY or CAD, however, they have different values and is more than anything else, an umbrella term used to describe hundreds of currencies.

Of them the most famous and the first to make it into the market of them all one that is most well-known and renowned, Bitcoin (BTC). It's still popular in its usage but it is also competing for the highest price. Altcoins are referred to as cryptocurrency that have been modeled on Bitcoin and offer minor changes on the platform, for instance, the use of specialized applications or processing speeds that are faster or more secure security.

Ethereum (ETH) is the most used altcoin currency in 2021 It is growing and is the most popular platform for a variety of NFTs and games on blockchain. It is able to provide a more targeted usage than Bitcoin because it's a complete platform (Ethereum) and also an exchange (Ether). It also means that games can be created and utilized on the blockchain.

These programs or games are known as decentralized apps (dapps) and constitute the most popular feature of this kind of currency. Ether is used to manage the dapps that are in the Ethereum platform. They can be traded as other cryptocurrency.

Another altcoin that is popular one is Litecoin (LTC). Litecoin utilizes "scrypt" evidence of working to keep their P2P decentralized network. This allows it to be maintained on computers with less power.

Another couple of most popular cryptocurrency include, however, they are not restricted to Polkadot (DOT), Cardano (ADA), Bitcoin Cash (BCH), Binance Coin (BNB), Solana (SOL) and Ripple's XRP (XRP).

The pros and cons of this shift to Crypto

The main "pro" to cryptocurrency is the fact that it is decentralized from the P2P networks. The fact that the blockchain is controlled by and for the public provides not just a high level of security and a difficult to hack and illicit transactions, but also the transparency further permits the system to monitor activity. This is why blockchain is open and traceable via encrypted data without losing its security. Furthermore, unlike physical money, crypto transactions can be conducted anywhere in the world , with practically no restrictions on the amount. Furthermore, these transactions typically take less than a single day and thus make it a viable option to bank. Additionally, transaction costs as well as interest rates or exchange rates of crypto are extremely affordable, and that is yet another benefit to crypto shifting over physical cash.

There are certain "cons" of the transition to cryptocurrency. These differ in intensity from the uniqueness to more serious issues that require attention. One of the biggest disadvantages to cryptocurrency is the fact that it's very energy-intensive. Due to the fact that it is the P2P network is huge and contains a lot of computers operating at high-power constantly, huge quantities of electricity are used to run it and is a very negative impact on the environment.

Socially, cryptocurrency is highly unstable and their value can fluctuate dramatically within just a few hours. There have been instances of investors putting all their savings in Bitcoin only to lose the entire amount. This is the reason why investors should not rely on cryptocurrency investments as their primary source of income. They should always be cautious and safe when it comes to their money since it is impossible to predict the future.

The technology behind cryptocurrency is continually getting improved and refined. More efficient technology, more effective algorithms, and a variety of ways to prove stakes are constantly being designed. The developers and crypto miners may be at odds with one with respect to issues that can lead to the split of the currency. This was the case with Bitcoin in the year it divided, resulting in Bitcoin Cash (BCH), that believed in increasing the block sizes of the blockchain between 1MB and 8MB with the intention of increasing the speed of transactions. When the cryptocurrency "forks" as this happens and splits, there is a risk that the price for the two competing currencies can be questioned and the investor has to decide if they wish to withdraw and change currencies, or prefer to go with the flow.

How Cryptocurrency as well as the Blockchain Are Using

Some businesses do not accept cryptocurrency as a means of payment, but as time passes increasing numbers of companies are willing accept it. In addition to being able to purchase goods and services as well, cryptocurrency is also able to be traded directly to the purchaser or via a third-party exchange broker. Coinbase or Kraken are two examples of third-party brokers that permit you to withdraw money following the cryptocurrency's deposit into them.

Particular to specific to the Ethereum platform, thanks to the various dapps and programs that can be integrated in it. marketplaces that are accessible via it, and which exclusively trade with ETH. The majority of NFTs are offered on these marketplaces. Other dapp categories are financial services, which allow you to lend tokens in exchange for interest or to borrow money as well as blockchain games where the player can play games and then sell assets in exchange for ETH and also technology where users earn ETH through surfing the Internet or leasing resources to build the capabilities of the platform.

What are we headed to?

In the process of converting Bitcoin's Bitcoin mining technology to Ethereum platform glitch was discovered where Ethereum required a faster processing speed, which is around 1 block/15 seconds , as in contrast to Bitcoin's 1 block/10 min. The standard mining system, which is known as"proof of work" draws lots of energy, consequently a new system known as proof of stake was designed. The use of "validators" to check blocks in the blockchain could eventually make Ethereum a more environmentally-friendly cryptocurrency than Bitcoin in the long run.

A major concern and long-standing issue in the cryptocurrency community is that the highly prized centralization and decentralization that is the P2P system could come at risk. For Ethereum particularly, the majority of blockchain mining is carried out by large businesses, employing hundreds of employees who dedicate their time and energy to the process. The process has been more centralized, which has ruined the goal of the system. And this is a problem.

One of the most difficult hurdles to overcome is the acceptance of society. There is a lot of skepticism about cryptocurrency's use, since rumors circulate regarding its use in crimes, but it is mostly due to the spreading of inaccurate information and the lack of widely accessible information about the field. When presented in a way that is not accurate, the concept of digital currency and blockchain might seem complicated, but the public is slowly getting to accept that it will be the new norm in.

Chapter 2: What Is The Metaverse?

The phrase "metaverse" was trending across the Internet since the announcement of Mark Zuckerberg of Facebook's rebranding as Meta. The apps of its affiliates such as some of the giants such as Instagram, Whatsapp, and Oculus VR, all have the Meta logo on their start-ups. Other areas that comprise the Internet are in a rage due to the mysterious and mechanical trailer that Zuckerberg declared the metaverse. The concepts behind it, even though they've been tried before in certain ways to virtual and augmented reality, appear so absurd and even absurd that it is hard not to laugh. If he does succeed together with other companies attracted by the concept and technology, the demand for the product is huge. Similar to Bitcoin was launched at a just 9 cents, beginning ventures in the world of metaverse hold the potential to explode over the long run.

A An In-depth Background of Meta and of the Metaverse

Meta

In the year 2004, Facebook was founded by Harvard University alumni Mark Zuckerberg, Eduardo Saverin, Dustin Moskovitz, Andrew McCollum, and Chris Hughes. The app had immediate impact within a short time: more than half of students in their undergraduate classes at their school had signed up to the app. The app grew its reach by the close of 2005, extending across and across the Western world, not just the U.S. One of the most important principles Zuckerberg made, and perhaps one of the main factors behind the network's success was the honesty the users. This meant that users were prohibited to lie about the identity of a person or any other aspect of one's personal life. as such, Facebook aimed to be an authentic way to determine what someone was doing. Another major benefit of the platform was the fact that it was absolutely free to sign up for an account, however the primary source of income for Facebook is via advertising, and this could result in privacy issues being discussed in the near future.

The year 2008 saw Facebook has surpassed MySpace to become the biggest social media platform in the Internet. Since the time it has grown to become a giant in the Internet as well as in society. Alongside individuals, the majority of businesses also started establishing accounts to increase the visibility for their business. Then, in 2012 Facebook became a publicly traded company which meant that users could buy shares in the company. The value of the company soared by several billion dollars in the following years.

Instagram, a major social media platform, which is more focused around short videos and pictures it was purchased from Facebook on April 12, 2012, for $1B cash and shares. Whatsapp was later bought by Facebook in the month of February for $14 billion and Oculus was purchased one month later for $2 billion, Zuckerberg obviously seeing the potential for VR as well as social networking opportunities.

On October 28, 2021 Mark Zuckerberg announced a major change in the name of his business, previously known as Facebook, and rebranded as Meta Platforms. This doesn't mean that any of the platforms within the company will change their names, but only that the company's parent. The primary reason behind this change is the long-term goals for the metaverse project in which complete digital immersion will be attained. There is however an idea that the change in name has as an additional goal distract attention away from the controversy that has been enshrined to this Facebook name, such as the selling and mining of information about consumers to companies that are interested in using it to create a personalised advertising strategy, hoping to be linked to a new project of growth. These scandals have brought Facebook into the spotlight as the poster child for infringing on privacy and bad technology practices. of privacy via social media. With the change of name to Meta media outlets, news organizations and Internet experts believe that Facebook is making an false promise to change the name and the new logo however, the same bad actions they expect will be the result of the announcement.

But, when it comes to the idea of a world of the metaverse Zuckerberg declares in the presser: "Over time, I believe we will be perceived as a metaverse business and I'd like to put our mission and identity to what we're building toward," (Thomas, 2021).

The Metaverse Metaverse

In 1992, one year after the beginning of the Internet the author Neal Stephenson released his science fiction novel titled "Snow Crash." The book is the source of Mark Zuckerberg's new brand, since the book describes a virtual that is distinct from reality and where the experience remains real. Both worlds are connected in the book, so that the event that occurs--for example, the drug "Snow Crash" was consumed in the "metaverse," it would be affecting the person who is actually. That's why Zuckerberg's metaverse, a real-life 3D immersive experience in which users can perform almost anything in a virtual space such as working, playing or even social gatherings.

VR and AR (AR as well as VR) are not brand new concepts. There have been a variety of approaches to the metaverse idea through different platforms and games. The most well-known games include: Minecraft, Fortnite, and Roblox. In these games, the player is able to be whoever they want to be and is not restricted to any degree by the boundaries. This means they are capable of going anywhere they want, and take any actions they wish to in accordance with the restrictions built in the game. The examples above are also multi-player, which means that the possibilities can be multiplied by the addition of additional players from the same world which allows them to interact exactly as they do in real-life, only it's notreal; it's virtual reality. In these games, gamers are able to simulate their lives without the stress of reality.

Meta already has a few features that are expected to be maintained throughout the Metaverse. The acquisition in 2014 from the business Oculus is an instance of a move towards virtual reality, specifically in their primary product: VR headsets. The device is placed over the user's eyes, and transforms their entire vision into a virtual world. Microsoft has also expressed an enthusiasm for the creation and expansion of this metaverse. They have been working on Extended Reality Projects (XR) that would feature virtual reality technology and avatars in their video and social conference services: Microsoft Teams. Other companies that are owned by Microsoft that are pursuing the metaverse include Minecraft, Xbox, and Skype. Microsoft has also collaborated together with U.S. Army to develop VR headsets that assist in the training of soldiers.

In all of these ways humanity isn't too far away from reaching the realm of the metaverse. The distinction between physical and the virtual worlds is more blurred due to the rise of cryptocurrency. It all started at the end of 2008 when Bitcoin released its release of the whitepaper on Bitcoin followed by 2009 with the official launch. We've all heard about cryptocurrency from the previous chapter, but what we've not talked about is the implications of it for creating the virtual world but you could probably put some connections already. First, the digitalization of money puts more dependence on the maintenance of the web-based realm. There's no requirement for banks or transactions that are regulated by the government for paying cryptocurrency. The metaverse is a place where it's likely that this will be the most common kind of currency that is accepted. In a different way it is that it is possible that the Ethereum platform already is like certain elements in the world of metaverse. Dapps can be directly programmed on the blockchain, making it an ideal marketplace for selling and buying artwork, digital assets, services and information video game inventory and many more.

The metaverse is expected to be in the process of being tested and use by 2035. That's not as far away as it seems This is due to all the ways that technology like the Internet is already working towards the idea as we have previously described. It is also speedier due to the fact that it will not only be Meta who are developing the project. every developer and business that creates AR and VR will be involved and put under the umbrella that is"the "metaverse." That means that there won't be multiple metaverses, all that is in line with the ideas from Stephenson, Zuckerberg, and similar visionaries are a part of the metaverse.

In his letter of founding for Meta, Zuckerberg (2021) declares:

We've moved from desktops through web to mobile, from text to pictures to videos. However, this isn't yet the final story. In the next stage, we will make it more immersive. [...]. The metaverse is what we call it that will affect every product we develop. The most important quality for the world of metaverses will be the feeling of being in a state of mind, like you're in the same space with another person or somewhere else. Being able to feel completely present with another is the ultimate goal of technology that connects people. That's why we're determined to create this.

The impact of the announcement

Zuckerberg's vision for the future has been made explicit to the masses that he wants to assist in the creation of a virtual world in which users can experience a full VR experience. The anticipated impact on society, technology environmental and finance will be addressed in Chapter 3 but there are already ripples of changes that were created by the announcement.

The general public is unsure whether it is prepared for this kind of integration in their daily lives The subject could be controversial, depending on the individuals involved in the debate. For starters, users who already use metaverse-like technology , like interconnected games or networks are probably not worried about this change. People who are less familiar with the inner workings of the Internet or those who worry that people will lose the ability to exist in the real world are very concerned. In light of the recent influx of kids who are obsessed with their electronic gadgets and gaming that they can't distinguish reality from fiction Many parents and senior citizens also doubt the utility of such tools and wonder if they will ever forget that they are more than a tool.

Furthermore, there are people who can't forget Mark Zuckerberg's record of success in his companies. Privacy concerns and Internet security are not uncommon because

25

Facebook has been known for selling user information to businesses to help them tailor their ads. The COVID-19 epidemic is a prime example. Facebook was also seen to not be concerned about the spreading of false information about security, medically approved treatments, and available vaccines available on their platform.

In the opinions of other tech-savvy people who are developers, designers, and enthusiastic consumers of virtual reality the launch that the world was metaverse-based appeared to be more than anything else, an attempt to take credit from existing products as an attempt to be a last-minute addition to the metaverse movementthat was thriving for the last decade prior to the involvement of Zuckerberg. The current metaverse technology developed from smaller companies were based by the same principle of decentralization, similar to cryptocurrencies which means that they do not have a central power and they are therefore not subject to the central control Meta's version could possess. However there are some who are happy about the momentum the announcement is likely to give to the movement and also the ways that technology can advance by the amount of money being committed to it by large corporations.

In terms of environmental criteria, whether metaverse platforms that are decentralized or centrally controlled are gaining popularity, they require massive amounts of energy. In the present, NFTs, mostly sold on Ethereum, are sold on the Ethereum blockchain, have been subject to intense criticism for the enormous carbon emissions to which they are linked, since for the receipt for an art work, enormous amounts of cryptocurrency mining needs to be done over a half million computers. This is to be performed to keep the blockchain updated. The carbon impact of these transactions however, is a subject of debate, because different sources of energy can be utilized to power computers. It is estimated that approximately 70 percent of the energy generated is clean, thereby reducing the environmental impact. But, in order to ensure sustainability over the long run the remaining 30% needs to be taken care of and solutions developed.

In spite of all the criticism however, there is one thing sure: The development and application in the realm of metaverses is a ongoing project that has been undertaken since the past few decades, by a variety of small and large businesses The announcement of Facebook's involvement along with plans for other major corporations to create their own versions of the metaverse, has drawn interest in the possibilities which it could bring.

Chapter 3: The Metaverse As It Is Metaverse

The metaverse aims to improve our lives, connecting individuals more than ever before and changing how people perform their jobs, play and interact. The fact that this technology is relatively new become a reality can be extremely daunting, but it is imperative to fully embrace -- and profit from the coming future. The idea is even more complicated as it is still developing. In certain ways the metaverse has already started with interactive games and crypto marketplaces However, in other ways, such as in the world of VR and AR which aren't yet widely used There is an extensive way to go. The ultimate goal, on which everyone will agree is for the metaverse to be able to function as an enhanced alternative to the Internet. If we look at the anticipated effects of the metaverse's incorporation into our daily lives when it is finally able to fully establish itself, we can take note of where we , as a species, are heading.

Technological Impact

The metaverse stands on the top of the pyramid of virtual and AR technology. Numerous companies that are involved in developing it with regard to hardware, have in mind VR headsets AR glasses and other similar technologies that will fully immerse the user into the experience. In lieu of sitting in a video call such as a video call users would be transported to a virtual, 3D meeting room in which all participants, depicted as avatars, could behave in the same way as they would actually in the same room.

This gaming industry is among the most eminent mediums that grasps the concept of the metaverse. It has used it multiple times on many platforms, including PC console, mobile phone as well as VR headsets. In the near future it is likely to see an evolution towards more extensive use of games on headsets. Maybe we will see new buildings that are designed to accommodate VR rooms. They will allow players to move around and play games without fear of hitting or breaking the real world objects.

Metaverse technology, due to how immersive it has to be to be usable for the average consumer will also need to evolve and grow exponentially over the years to come prior towards its release. Broadband speeds need to be more efficient than ever before, with over 1GB/sec to provide an immersive experience (Vena 2021). It may sound impossible however, every day, technology becomes ever more realistic to the point that Disney creates movie scenes using avatars that look like they are from real actors, and once they're developed, the software is already outdated.

This brings us to the next issue software. Microsoft for instance, has been working on Mesh in the Microsoft Teams app, which will bring avatar holograms onto the platform. This is just a initial step toward integrating holograms into metaverse-focused apps.

Economic Impact

The economic impact of the metaverse could be divided into two different areas. There is of course the rise in the use of cryptocurrency that is anticipated, because this is the principal method through which goods are distributed across the world of digital. A different economic impact is the modernization of online shopping and retail platforms. In addition, there are new products that are coming out and be sold, while ten many years ago, these items could not be considered important items.

We've covered cryptocurrency in depth as well as the stigma created by myths about rampant crime because of its absence in central authorities. The real nature of cryptocurrency is the existence of vibrant digital marketplaces such as Ethereum and other platforms. The metaverse is expected to behave similarly and may even be more appealing to consumers than the currently online shopping. For instance, NFTs are sold on Ethereum and what the buyer will get is basically a document proving the ownership of a portion. People often dismiss this type of business since they aren't aware of the value of it, but when you consider the world of the metaverse it could seem more sensible for these people. In a completely digital world the NFT can be displayed in a virtual space or even charge crypto currency for viewing the exhibit similar to art exhibits or actual art purchases that are made in real life.

In addition, online and retail shopping platforms could benefit from the metaverse revolution because they offer an enhanced online experience which means that their customers can be reached to a greater extent than possible. To help visualize this idea an online store might be able to use holographic and avatar tech to demonstrate to consumers what clothing items could appear like on their body including height and size as well. The customer would no longer be making a bet on the clothes they purchase when they place an order, thereby encouraging greater purchases for the company. The existence of this kind of online shopping experience is crucial due to COVID-19 is a pandemic and a better system for this will be greatly welcomed by the majority of people. Since the year 2000, in fact the majority of people were exposed to shopping online for the first time, this market is now ripe for development to keep pace in line with the times and remain in the water.

Additionally new products and opportunities for business will be created due to the growth of the metaverse. With the emerging virtual reality technology, where users can be themselves as avatars and create an online market of cryptocurrency for various clothes or styles which can be used for personalization, similar to the fashion market in reality. Other ventures in business are bound to be created especially for developers and coders to build different applications or websites in the virtual world.

Social Impact

Similar to similar to Internet like the internet, the metaverse will be governed and maintained according to the way society shapes it. It is ultimately the community that will sit at the center of technology. With this new digital platform, innovative solutions for common areas are possible. the interconnectedness between individuals will be greater than ever before, as will more widespread acceptance of the general technological advancement, despite being new and scary for some, particularly with science fiction novels such as Snow Crash or Ready Player One which depict technologically driven, dystopian environments.

In the beginning, thanks to the metaverse, real-life industries are becoming more accessible to the general public. We've already talked about the ways in which e-commerce is changing and other industries will also experience significant improvements. For instance, in the area of education for instance, the customer can learn the theories of evolution through the virtual character that is Charles Darwin, and be transported to the Galapagos Islands from the comfort of their home. Another scenario is that you could be among the crowd at Martin Luther King Jr.'s famous "I Have A Dream" speech, and also learn what the movement for civil rights was like within the United States. Additionally education is not the only area of society to change. In the field of healthcare as an example the application in the form of AR and VR may increase the effectiveness of medical equipment and procedures. They are also beginning to be utilized for the education of first responders. There are numerous ways that metaverse technology can benefit humanityand provide options are still to be created.

The most likely next phase of the Metaverse as it relates to social changes is an increase in communication between humans. Thanks to social media, the Internet and the social network, people are able to write or talk to each others from all over the globe in just a few seconds. But with the metaverse the users will be able to communicate with each others more easily within a 3-dimensional space in which their interactions will feel like being sharing a room. It's like what games that are based on the metaverse are playing right currently, like Minecraft or Roblox, which is proving how this tech and its future isn't that distant as it might appear. Actually, Meta has made this innovative method for presenting the social network their primary focus since the name change to Facebook.

As time goes on as time passes, a consensus among the public of the benefits that the metaverse could and will bring humanity will develop. With sufficient resources such as books videos, articles, and articles that explain what the metaverse is the future will see people abandon the fear of being technological slaves and accept it as an integral aspect of their daily lives that are designed to make their lives simpler, more efficient. It will also eliminate false information about the technology that is already developed, and also providing information on cryptocurrencies which will become the main source of currency in the future.

The metaverse is likely to become more creator-centric in the future as this project will bring together to the whole world and through the help of experienced developers and small businesses keep a system that is decentralized designed for and for the people. There are some issues that could be a part of this, as tension is brewing between investors and creators. As is evident in the current NFT world Some artists are not satisfied that their work could be purchased as tokens and later resold. But, generally speaking similar to how anybody can build an online video, website or game and publish it online, the same will be in the metaverse, possibly with directly coding for blockchain to allow these games to be linked to cryptocurrency. This way, the creators will become the mainstay in the world of metaverse.

Environmental Impact

Environmental impacts are the inevitable consequence of most initiatives and inventions. For the metaverse, there's positive impact including a reduction in transportation, the creation of more sustainable energy employment, as well as the avoiding of potentially dangerous situations through virtual training. However, the same issues that can be observed with the electricity requirements of blockchain processing and mining could be seen in the metaverse, which could be viewed as environmental pitfalls. In all likelihood it is also the possibility that any future efforts to protect the planet, along with technological innovation and advancement with sustainability in mind could alter the path we're on , and give society to benefit from both the real and virtual world.

How can the metaverse assist the planet? In the first place, the more people meet and work on an interactive virtual space it will reduce the amount of a need to move into a physical workspace. For the typical 9-to-5 office job, the majority of tasks will be done online, allowing the worker to perform their job from the convenience of their home. There is also the possibility that complete metaverse-integrated jobs will appear, having to do with maintenance of the crypto marketplace and possibly even sustainability-centered technological research positions. Additionally, hazardous and inefficient workplace training can be completed online in order to reduce the environmental footprint of job-related activity, which will not be required anymore.

However, there are a few environmental issues related to the creation of the metaverse as well as its care. As previously mentioned, in the past that cryptocurrency mining as well as NFT transactions require massive amounts of electricity that can result in an increase in carbon emissions globally. For Metaverses, these same principles apply: it is a power-hungry system which is why it requires a fast processing speed. Researchers from the University of Massachusetts have found that the most common AI algorithms of present time emit up to 626,000 pounds. of carbon dioxide in order to be taught (GlobalData Thematic Research 2021). Researchers at Lancaster University say that, in the event that the industry of video games is transformed into a metaverse-like platform that is cloud-based, as it currently stands, by 2030 it will result in an increase of 30% in carbon dioxide emissions resulting from gaming.

At the very end of the day, there's still the possibility of a solution. No one can anticipate the direction of technological advancements or sustainable developments however, to address a problem, society has to be aware of the issue. This is why it's essential to understand the facts and collaborate to solve the problem, as the metaverse can be a powerful source of economic, social technological and technological advances however, it wouldn't be feasible without the ability to maintain a healthy balance with reality and the environment , which is the lifeblood for all of us.

Chapter 4: What Augmented Reality Is: How

It Will Function In The Metaverse

You've probably heard about the Pokemon Go craze of 2016 that involved catching monster-like creatures, which were transposed by smartphone cameras onto real-world surfaces. Perhaps they've used to use the Google Lens feature on their Android mobile phone to find what the names of specific animal, plant or insect which they found in the woods that surround their home. These are only a few of the common illustrations of ways that the concept of augmented realities, or AR has been able to be integrated into our daily lives over the past decade. At its heart, the concept behind AR is to capture the reality and overlay virtual elements onto it, for example, to improve or augment it.

In the future the concept of AR is likely to be even more popular than it is currently. In actuality, games like Pokemon Go and apps like Google Lens would fit in perfectly as metaverse technology. In this section, the workings of Augmented Reality will be explained in depth along with the steps to be taken to realize the full AR potential and how AR could benefit humanity and the metaverse and its time-line.

What is Augmented Reality?

Augmented reality is made up of the hardware as well as software. The hardware that is used for AR typically ranges from the standard phone, PC or tablet to specialized devices made to work with specific software. The user is usually able to hold the device they are using towards a surface and it will recognize whatever is on the surface using computer vision technology to ensure that images superimposed onto it will be correctly placed.

An excellent modern-day example is filters that are available on social media platforms such as Snapchat as well as Instagram. All you have to do is hold the camera in front of their face, and by using camera technology their features such as the eyes, nose the mouth, eyebrows and the mouth are all recognised. The application can then superimpose AR by using the camera's lens for example, such as expanding the eyes, putting dogs' ears on top of the head creating an animation to play when the mouth opens, etc.

Hardware

The equipment required to run AR is cameras, by which the actual-world image as well as virtual elements are observed in a live camera feed. In addition to the camera, other essential components include GPS (Global Location System) and microphones, processor and display. Through the years there have been numerous specific systems developed to support AR. Of the more intriguing models is SixthSense technology, which was announced in 2009 by the MIT Media Lab's Fluid Interfaces Group. The prototype was rough comprising everyday items like mirrors, smartphones small projector, as well as cameras.

The projector projects an image. And by using fingers that are colored thumb caps worn by the user to cameras, elements of the image can be moved by simply the movements of fingers and hands. Any surface that the projector could be projected would be able to be interactive. The SixthSense technology is just one of the ways that technology could be tailored in the near future to support high-quality AR experiences.

Another, perhaps more advanced and more complete product is the Microsoft Hololens. This is a real headset that has been designed with sensors and optics that detect objects in real life and allow users be able to engage with virtual holograms the front of them.

Software

Software is possibly the most significant aspect in making an AR product. And, in reality it's unlikely for the majority of people to buy special equipment as soon as the metaverse is released, as it's a relatively new concept to a lot of. Thus, AR had to find ways to be able to work with the devices that people already have: smartphones. Snapchat, Instagram, Pokemon Go along with Google Lens are software apps specifically designed for phones and have gained immense popularity with the majority of people.

We've already proven that augmented reality is based on computer vision. Live feeds from cameras are displayed by the gadget, which determines 3D location, depth of view, and the direction of objects that are in focus. Registration tools, like motion sensors, determine the areas where virtual images may be superimposed. Machine learning algorithms determine where items are situated within the real world , and can track the objects as they move in the camera's view. All these elements are displayed in the output device which will display an end-to-end AR feed.

Different types of AR

There are many methods that augmented reality could perform. One of them is "marker-based AR." It is an app created by a user specially developed to detect a particular object, also known as a "marker." This can be done with QR codes, logos or recognition.

There's also the complete opposite of AR based on markers, which is called markers-free AR. There aren't any markers in this case and the camera cannot detect any specific object. Instead it is a virtual 3D object could be projected onto a rendered space. Some examples of how this type of AR is used are the arrangement of furniture in virtual space to show a space that is furnished in a space that is not being used or the orientation to a digital image within the palms of hands.

The final type of popular AR technology is known as "projector-based AR." This is similar to it is like the SixthSense prototype was described earlier and the AR is based more on the real worldby creating hologram-like images of objects. Practically speaking, this kind of augmented reality is utilized in light guide systems.

The Developer's Perspective

So , how can people and businesses create code for AR technology? First, with the case of marker-based AR programming, it is cheap and simple when compared to other forms of AR. The reason is that the camera is looking for something specific that is usually different from the world.

In the case of markerless AR the majority of power is dispersed to the phone. It also has a slow rendering speed, as there's more work to be completed with the phone than markers-based AR. It also relies on flat surfaces that are textured (Schechter 2020).

Then, with projection-based AR the process gets more complex. The method uses projection mapping, which means that projections are required to create an electronic overlay on different surfaces. It requires understanding that goes beyond camera devices and camera vision tech however, it also requires knowledge of the projection hardware.

How Can We Achieve Full AR?

Many ways, the basis for the AR world has been laid. There's a wealth of technology created that works well in modern times. There are however enhancements that need to be made and they will be feasible with the rise of the metaverse, and all the attention it will receive from developers and users alike.

The first thing to be aware of is that creating and coding Augmented Reality programs isn't an easy task. Computer vision technology is actually an entire area of development and research. Although it is easy for human eyes to scan an camera's lens and determine the contents of the feed computer systems have a difficult at doing this, so finding ways to get computers to process this information and render it into a form is a hot subject that is being researched thoroughly however the advancements have been incredibly impressive so far. The ability to fully utilize AR will have a lot to do with improving this technology , and also synchronizing it with real-time motion. When playing AR games such as Pokemon Go, for example there won't be any jittering or vibration of the holograms caused due to the sensitivity of motion sensors.

Furthermore, the goal of achieving complete AR could mean a total integration to social media. The one of Zuckerberg's major goals to transform Facebook through the lenses of the metaverse is through creating avatars that are superimposed on real people, which users can alter and alter their appearance through digital enhancements in the way they'd like. For instance If someone wanted to have a Giraffe head and wanted to add the head by using AR technology and move around. Those who are on Facebook could view the avatar's virtual appearance through their camera.

Social media isn't the only area that augmented reality could penetrate and completely transform the business. The applications of AR in various sectors like office, healthcare and education have been covered within Chapter 3. The complete AR integration is yet another illustration of how technology might achieve its full potential in the near future, if the technology continues to be improved in order to assist in the search for new strategies and solutions to old problems, such as teaching the next generation or educating new workers efficiently. In terms learning and teaching the next generations, the concept that enhanced learning through visual stimulation is backed by some scientific research to back it. It is estimated that 80 or 90% an individual's knowledge is derived from their visual (Porter and Heppelmann 2017b).

The benefits in an AR World

The AR world is going to greatly benefit humanity this is the reason the metaverse is based on its ideas and technologies behind VR (or virtual reality). The benefits for healthcare as well as education sectors of AR within the actual world and the particular applications for AR will be discussed as well.

Healthcare

In the health sector in the healthcare industry, products that utilize AR technology can be utilized to show internal features and help new employees learn. For visualizing internal features it is possible to use the case using AccuVein technology. AccuVein detects the patterns of heat within the veins of a patient and overlays the patterns onto the patient, making it possible for the medical professional to identify an area of interest within the circulation system. Because of the use of this type of technology, needle sticks that work in the first attempt have increased by up to 45% (Porter and Heppelmann 2017b). This reduces the frequency associated with "escalations," which is when the situation becomes worse because of the use of a needle that is not correct. When it comes to training new employees Augmented reality could teach workers step-by-step how to accomplish specific tasks, giving workers who are full-time to be able to concentrate on their work instead of offering constant support for trainees.

Education

The benefits that the educational system could reap from AR lead to a single conclusion

Visual representation of education concepts can increase retention of many students who consider this their primary method to learn. The reason for this is due to each person's unique cognitive load. It relates to their capacity to accomplish mental tasks. Learning, when information is attempted to enter an intellectual load initially traverses an intellectual distance that is the period between the moment that information is presented and when the brain processes it and comprehends it. When compared to audible or written information, visualisation has been proven to be the most efficient method of reducing cognitive distance for the majority of people. This is the reason AR is so exciting for education systems.

Furthermore, AR has the added benefit of interactivity. Being capable of interacting with buttons, knobs and so on. are fantastic instruments for learning kinesthetics and can further expand the capabilities of technology in teaching new generations.

Military

Training for military personnel and the use of AR was briefly discussed in Chapter 2. In the first place, in-person training can be costly and requires a shared schedule of time for both the instructor and student and the knowledge isn't always understood in the first attempt by the trainee. The military utilizes AR to provide a safe method to replicate combat for training purposes and has been one of the initial and most enthusiastic adopters of this kind of technology. Examples of equipment used include helmet-mounted displays and intelligent glasses (Bonson and Chandler, n.d.).

The head-mounted displays of augmented reality transcend the basic training of the military. For instance, these AR displays could be used for surveillance of a particular terrain to create virtual blueprints or satellite views that a soldier can use to stay clear of any danger.

Chapter 5: Risks And Challenges

Like with all big, new idea there will be challenges that come up either directly or indirectly. When it comes to the growing metaverse and the desire to be an integral part of it there are a few risks and challenges must be aware. Certain of these risks are like the issues we have seen in the world of Internet or social media while others are entirely new. For those who are looking for challenges, the developers will encounter a variety of difficulties in constructing the technology this revolutionary platform needs to seamlessly integrate its way in the daily lives of populace, as the Internet was able to do a few years ago.

Social Risk

Addiction

With the rapid advancement of the digital age, many people -- and particularly, children, find themselves attracted to technology. Therapists are now dealing with thousands of kids who, on a variety of levels, so deeply engrossed in their devices that, in some degree, they can't be able to live their lives regularly. The advent of the Internet and all the benefits it brought however, came new issues which include the issue of addiction. The question is whether Internet Addiction Disorder (IAD) is considered to be a real mental illness is still a hot topic of discussion.

In the year 2016, Common Sense Media, an organization that is non-profit and designed to review films and technology for families, learned in a survey that about 50% of teens were "addicted" towards their smartphones and that 75% of individuals felt the desire to instantly respond to messages (Robb 2016,). However, most users would not use the term "addiction" to describe themselves in the exact same way that addiction to drugs can make an individual chemically addicted through altering brain. True addiction is the ability to remove all other things from a person's life, and not being capable of functioning normally physically or socially and requiring an ever-growing quantity of the drug as time passed. It is less common with regards to the Internet and that's why it's often not categorized as being the cause of "addiction."

There are kids who are severely affected by the quantity of screen-time they are exposed to. Many children are admitted to therapy centers because they are unable to discern the difference between what's real and what's virtual. But, it is disputed whether or not the results are actually due to access to the world of the internet, as they may also be suffering from various other issues or disorders that were not screened for and, when combined with screen time has led to light new signs. In any case, the most effective method of understanding a child that the parent believes spends too much time in technology is to seek out experts in the field of psychology and child therapy.

Why are games, media, and apps so addictive? It's because of nature; the longer players spend playing on an website, the more money it may earn from ads, purchases in app or through other means. Video game companies typically make "compulsory loops" that cause players to desire to play on and on. The anticipation, which leads to rewards triggers dopamine levels in the brain, which can make the player feel happy and makes users wanting to use this technology (Smith, n.d.). The types of rewards that can be rewarded could include the completion of a particular level in an online game, or gaining "likes" on the social media page to show some kind of confirmation. The uncertainty and dependence on the user's performance to attain these rewards can make the experience more thrilling which increases dopamine.

The metaverse intends to transform technology into something more interactive and more real than it has ever been. It will not only enhance social media usage but also encourage users to spend more time of time on their platforms, which is more than the current Internet. Thus, there is the risk of chance of a growing dependence on technology, specifically by young people who's minds are in a state of development and mold. This poses the social threat of the next generation that won't be capable of functioning outside of reality as effortlessly as those who didn't have virtual or Augmented Reality integrated into their childhood.

The subject becomes more complicated in debates is this an issue in the business, which purposefully creates a culture of addiction in order to maintain users engaged? Or is this issue, instead of placing burden on the metaverse, or the Internet as a whole, a part of parental control? It is after all the parents who decide on how the amount of screen time a child gets and it is the parents who purchase the gadgets. In this manner it's possible to debate that parents are responsible for how their children interact with technology.

Social Media

Looking at what the next phase of metahumanism holds the world of social media is only getting better in terms of interaction and accessible than ever before. But, as we've said addiction is also likely to be more prevalent. Furthermore, there's the challenge of successfully transferring an already huge and well-established user database to a completely new platform. Additionally, many of the issues that modern social media has to face, including security or privacy concerns cannot be solved simply by advancing the technology used as well as changing the brand name for the business.

First , the addictive nature of social media has been discussed; the concept is "likes" on posts releasing dopamine for the account's owner. But, unlike iPad games, or watching films and videos social media has an extremely strong social aspectthat brings people from all over the globe who might not otherwise have had the chance to meet and also giving them the opportunity to communicate about their ideas, exchange opinions and learn from one another. In this instance the issue at hand is not one that is easy to overcome. The concept of FOMO which is fear of missing out is a growing concern, as people believe they must keep track of all the experiences of their acquaintances, in the fear of being in the dark about some interesting thing. In the future, when there will be more to discover, FOMO sentiments will definitely continue to grow.

The problem of moving an existing user base to a different platform will be explained within the developer's challenges portion of this article, but it is a risk to society that the metaverse must take on. In the most moment, Meta is already seeing difficulties with its rebranding. Their primary site, Facebook is still the primary face of the company so currently there is no connection between Mark Zuckerberg with the word "Meta" even if they do or even in a humorous sense. Similar things was seen previously with another large firm, Google, which, in 2015, changed its name to the parent company Alphabet, Inc. In the hope of expanding beyond being an actual search engine. Similar to Meta but for the public at large it is often known as Google because the majority of consumers do not have a concern for the bureaucracy that runs the company.

The last issue is that the issues social media currently face could be exacerbated by the advent of the Metaverse. Facebook was in the news when it announced its rebranding to Meta in the wake of numerous critics who suggested that this change was because of the stigma that the name carries. Facebook was infamous for selling personal data of their users to huge companies to provide targeted, personal advertisements. The whole thing was done under the false claim that users would be in control of the way their data was used by filtering options. This is why the world was abuzz when Facebook changed its name and appeared to be a straightforward process of changing the name to allow it to shield itself from negative news without making any fundamental modifications. How can one thus expect companies to act any differently--especially when it pays so handsomely--when the metaverse will just require even more personal information from users, as it truly becomes a virtual self.

This isn't the only issue associated with social media, which will eventually be transferred into the metaverse. Internet security is a concern for many since the first time it was made available. The fact that people can appear to be who they are is terrifying Anyone with whom you interact online may be totally different in real life from what they portray in. With Facebook there are measures implemented to avoid this from happening at all cost as it erodes the very principles upon the basis of which it was built, by checking every account to ensure that they are managed by real people , who provide their true information. This is, as has been discussed, a different matter however, it does work to block from bot-run accounts. Other metaverse platforms can't be expected to follow the same precautions in the same way as Facebook, and that raises the question: what if you are enticed by an holographic character that is real within the virtual world and then discover that the account is fake by a malicious motive, it will be more destructive and harder to find than in the present Internet.

Environmental Risk

The risk to the environment of the metaverse is blockchain mining. One of the most important concerns of developers is finding the best way to completely base their process on renewable, clean, and green energy, if they are the intention of bringing their vast-reaching vision to fruition.

The Developers' Challenge

Engineering and Coding

There have seen significant developments not just in sandbox environments, such as games such as Minecraft or Roblox as well as in AR and cryptocurrency dapps. Platforms such as Ethereum allow direct programming straight into the blockchain. However, this method of blockchain programming isn't very well-known or widespread in recent times. Blockchain coding is difficult , and that developers need to face their moral responsibilities regarding the negative aspects associated with their job are just a few dangers that the metaverse has to overcome in order to develop.

The Internet is on the verge of becoming the Next Internet

In order to into the next larger and better Internet and to achieve the ultimate purpose for all of this metaverse discussion There are many obstacles to overcome. One of the biggest is that of moving existing users to a new platform that is completely different taking into account the demographics of the databases. Other challenges include maintaining the platform as independent, which can lead to interoperability and financial problems.

Facebook is still the most used social media platform, as of 2021. However, fewer young people who are under 18 are joining. The age range of 19 to about 25 is the largest and it decreases as you get older, however it was discovered that a lot of users of middle age or more create accounts every day. Because Facebook has evolved to be more mature-oriented generally there's a chance of sudden changes particularly when you consider that VR demographics, the ones who really excites them, are mostly young adults (Digital on the Move 2021). The majority of Facebook users feel comfortable with the current Facebook look and it's hard to imagine them accepting a total change in the normal.

Another issue that the creators of the metaverse confront is the age-old battle of digital communities to keep the system uncentralized. With so many companies understanding the potential and value of the opportunities in the metaverse, to ensure balance there can be no single authority or authority over that virtual playground.

The concept of decentralization comes interoperability. This is an important technological advance that is required to create the foundations of a functioning metaverse. Interoperability is the concept of a user being able to switch between different apps using the same profile and avatar. This requires an effort by developers from all metaverse projects as they have to find a way for users to travel between platforms while keeping the same profile.

In the end, the metaverse is costly. If certain virtual worlds wish to appear realistic to appeal to those who are first-time buyers The cost in digital currency is expensive. This could be the reason why the involvement of large a company as Meta could be significant for a portion people who are interested in the metaverse. It is an important source of money. However, financial challenges present a barrier to those who would be eager to attempt in the field of programming to build an upcoming platform. There's a lot to do to make real-life social avatars to communicate in a manner that is not as artificial and also. For platforms already in existence such as Second Life, player avatars don't offer the same level of freedom as real people do because every action must be encoded and animated. To get closer to life-likeness, programming and animating budgets are likely to get more costly as well.

Chapter 6: The Main And Coming Projects

We are getting closer to the conclusion of the general information about the metaverse, Meta as well as cryptocurrency-related projects. In order to provide you with all that you need to know about where technology is headed, we'll look at the top applications that are driving the industry to the metaverse. They include social networks and video games.

Minecraft, Roblox, and Fortnite

Minecraft, Roblox, and Fortnite are three hugely popular games played by young people of the last decade. Each easily fits as the top three most played games in 2021 and beyond, with Minecraft being the top-selling game of all time with 234 million sold (GamingSection 2020).

The attraction to these games particularly Minecraft and Roblox is that there isn't a real goal or reason behind it. Although there is a massive marketplace for RPGs and narrative-based games with Minecraft and Roblox players continue to play because what makes the game enjoyable is the players' involvement. In Minecraft the player can choose to play in a "Survival" game mode or single player or multiplayer, in which players basically play as the hero of a pristine and uniqueworld that is generated randomly. In this universe, players need to collect resources to survive. Even though there is technically a final game, players are able to play, build, and behave however they like and that's why they usually continue to play in that world after they've completed all of the main "goals" which the game put for them. In the alternative game mode Minecraft has to offer, "Creative" mode, players are granted unlimited resources. In essence, the player "plays God" in the world, with the ability to construct or destroy anything and travel anywhere in the world. There's no reason to play this mode of play apart from letting imagination and imagination dictate what the player decides to do.

There's more to play with in Minecraft and Roblox because of community involvement. Players who are invested in the game can create public servers with their own unique set of rules and guidelines, as well as stories or minigames ready to be enjoyed by the general public. They can also make money from the players by offering a variety of benefits that can be purchased. This idea, as one might recognize, very closely resembles the ideals of the metaverse, but at the smaller scale. One central account can connect to hundreds of decentralized different-led worlds that are entirely created by crowds and funded by the crowd.

Fortnite's metaverse is a slightly different than the different games. It's mostly the battle royale kind of game where the players enter a realm that functions as an arena and must then battle to be the last remaining. This is the main gaming aspect. It is however, Tim Sweeney, the chief executive for Epic Games that created Fortnite claims it is a metaverse game. Fortnite is a game that is metaverse as it includes non-gaming activities (Bradley 2021,). For instance, Fortnite has a variety of events in the game including concerts real artists have staged which were enjoyed by millions of gamers looking through the eyes of avatars on the platform.

Sandbox

Sandbox is a pioneer in Ethereum games that are blockchain-based, and is an interactive, world-building sandbox playground that is centered around creating and building art. It began as a game for mobile tablets and phones before expanding into the PC platform, too. It utilizes SAND currency, which is specific to the universe it is in. It allows players to purchase lots of land in the game and make virtual minigames or art galleries that sell NFTs for sale or charge to view. As a result they are firmly connected directly to NFT marketplace, which means that designers and artists benefit from the platform. Additionally, there are "Alpha passes" which are offered to just 5,000 individuals and give them the chance to participate in games to win SAND tokens (Ferrari 2021, Ferrari).

This game also is expected to be fully controlled by the crowd within the next few years and the developers hope to see it fully create its own economy using SAND. The user base in 2021 is more than 16,000 players. The Sandbox has partnered with numerous large corporations which all own lots of land to market their real-life business and products.

Second Life

Second Life, developed in 2003, was perhaps the first virtual world that has appear on the internet. By 2021, there were more than 1 million users in its virtual world. Second Life as with the other platforms mentionedabove, is an open-world, sandbox-style game. It doesn't have an objective, because players must determine how they would like to use it. It's different because This game isn't about creating. It's much more focused on connections and social interaction as opposed to the other games mentioned so far. Second Life boasts being used by numerous companies currently to host meetings and discussions. In less formal settings there are a variety of communities that have been established around the world, like musical clubs, group for roleplaying and virtual cinemas, to mention just a few.

The way Second Life makes money is through an online marketplace where customers can purchase and sell clothes pet, furniture and much many more items.

Second Life as a gaming platform also offers a valuable insight into the potential risks and issues that the metaverse could face due to its their resemblance to the concept. There have been problems that relate to the social component and the anonymity of the game as it's hard to control and maintain the power and in the hands of the players. There were virtual riots, with sexual content, which has not been totally prohibited, making it extremely sexually explicit as well as highlighting the issue barely discussed within Chapter 5, which is that If all the players are given the freedom to do what they wish online, it is inevitable that some will misuse the power.

VRChat

VRChat is an online social network which has been growing within the VR headset gaming community. It allows users who wears the headset, to explore and create new worlds, build avatars, connect with friends, and join groups all through a single platform. Through the experience of people who have played the app for hundreds of hours, they have uncovered some interesting observations about VR, which could differ from what those who hasn't or not used it in a long time may believe. One such finding was that, even though people may think that what that is the next step for VR is hyper-realistic graphics, amazing stunning worlds and avatars however, it is actually quite stressful for the brain. Users who are used to VR tend to prefer simpler graphics because they have more information that can be processed in a single session. VRChat clearly proves that there is a space for every kind of assets and art on the web.

Decentraland

Decentraland is one of the first fully open, decentralized game entirely controlled by its players. Similar to The Sandbox, it runs on the Ethereum blockchain but has the currency of its users, MANA for its marketplace. MANA serves as an official token. When modifications or updates are required to be made to the software an election system takes place for all users who have MANA. The types of votes taken include changes to policies and auctions for land and development subsidy and all with effects that are in-world. The usage of governing tokens serves to ensure that the decision-making process for the game entirely in the control of the players, so that developers don't become an unreliable power source in the games.

There is a different type of currency that is used in Decentraland in addition to MANA that is in reality the trading of specific NFTs, referred to as LAND. These serve as virtual plots of land. The primary purpose of the game is to acquire vacant plots of LAND to renovate them, create things on them and then sell the plots. Others can go to different plots and interact with one another through messages or voice chats, as well as moving. The game generally is an investment hub, where people could purchase LAND and then become the landlord, for instance that someone wishes to open a store due to of the location in game and coordinates of the area the owner must pay lease to the owner of that LAND. This is another method to earn money from the in-game NFTs. The general trend is that buying LAND is now quite costly because of its success with the most affordable plot of land as of December 2021 costing $4000, which is also due to the fact that there are only a few of plots that are available for purchase around the globe.

Decentraland comes in second place as the most-played game that is built using the

Ethereum blockchain. It's within the Top 3 with The Sandbox and Axie Infinity.

Axie Infinity

Axie Infinity has become the world's most played blockchain game in 2021 and is expected to continue growing. Contrary to The Sandbox or Decentraland, both games that are based around the use of NFTs as well as physical assets Axie Infinity is a combat game. It is a game where players are able to collect NFTs from small monsters that will then battle against the monsters of other players and are referred to as "Axies." But when compared to The Sandbox or other games it is now rather expensive to play because of its popularity that requires at least three axes to play, each of which costs several hundred dollars. In addition to Axies, players can also purchase items and land.

They can also be crossed, and offered on the market with love potions which can be grown, essential for breeding. In addition to market transactions there are many ways which players earn money. Participating in tournaments against other axies, like there are prizes to be won at stake.

The largest market, which accounts for 40 percent of the player base of Axie Infinity is the Philippines. For those who are from the Philippines, especially during the time of the COVID-19 epidemic the Philippines, being able to switch to online work in the decentralized, player-paid and game created by the players, instead of traveling abroad has been a huge benefit.

Star Atlas

Star Atlas is different from the other games on blockchain since it's not integrated into Ethereum. Instead, it operates on another cryptocurrency chain known as Solana (SOL) which is faster in processing transactions, and is available at lower price relative to Ethereum. Because of this, Solana as an alternative cryptocurrency is likely to become as well-known or even surpass Ethereum because it's still fairly new and was official launched in March of 2020.

The game is an NFT-based science fiction metaverse in which players are part of one of the factions and try to beat other players. Players accumulate resources, resolve problems, and embark on adventures.

Through the formation of small or large groups that are joined by other players There is the possibility of the creation of autonomous decentralized organisations (DAOs) that are able to govern their areas, on which they could develop cities or micro-economies. Any assets that players acquire in game are also resold by players, giving the player total control. This, in addition to the aim of decentralization and an entirely controlled by players, provides a reward in the form of money to participate.

Another way that Star Atlas differs from some other blockchain games is that it operates with two currencies the ATLAS token and POLIS. ATLAS tokens are the game's in-game economy, which allows for the purchase of goods and NFTs. In contrast, POLIS tokens are used to manage the game, meaning that those who own POLIS can make decisions regarding the development and updates. This is just one of the ways Star Atlas encourages decentralization, by giving its users the ability to shape the future of the company.

Meta: Facebook, Instagram, Whatsapp And More

We've all heard that Facebook is being rebranded as Meta Platforms now. This means that in the near future all social media firms that are part of the acquisition will shift to a metaverse-like view. For Facebook it is avatars that interact with one another in a virtual world. For other platforms such as Instagram or Whatsapp which are subsidiaries of Meta How will the situation alter?

It's not entirely certain. Even though Mark Zuckerberg has said that Meta will be a metaverse-focused business, there's an enormous number of users of Both Instagram and Whatsapp who might not be as accommodating to modifications. First, Instagram is primarily a platform for sharing photos, and therefore it isn't much of a advantage to moving to an immersive or virtual experience. Whatsapp is also unable to make sense in the metaverse because it's mostly messaging apps that's appeal is that people all over the globe and across various phones can communicate with each other with no worries about additional fees. The announcement is being fresh in the minds of people in the month of October 2021, there remain numerous unanswered questions that are yet to be revealed. One thing is for sure that Meta's Facebook being a major popular culture and the fact that the fact that it invests in the metaverse implies that massive transformation is likely in the coming years.

What can this teach us?

In general, certain aspects of all of the games and apps discussed are similar, enhancing the perception that people hold of the metaverse. In the first place, they all fall in that category known as "sandbox" game, in which the rules for the best places to go and what actions to take depend on what the player decides. Another commonality between these games is the fact that all of them have distinct marketplaces that are independent from the game, but allow it to develop its own economic. For blockchain games, these features are essential to the experience However, in games that are just proto-metaverses, such as Second Life or Minecraft, the purchase is merely a way to enhance the experience and not appropriate for everyone. NFTs have also taken into their own lives in addition to the art market on Ethereum and have proven their worth in different games, making them more accessible to a greater number of players.

Chapter 7: Essentials Of Investing In Crypto

With all the necessary information on the current and future state of technology and cryptocurrency, as well as the advancements of the Internet and the Internet, as well as details on the progress of the metaverse and the current projects that are in line with it, it's time to tackle the main question: How can you earn money from this? In this part of our book we'll look at the ways to identify areas you can invest, what amount of cash you can invest on investments, how to divide them and the best way to make your first investments.

How to Buy Your First Crypto

First, there are a lot of areas for investing in cryptocurrency. In Chapter 1 there are a myriad of different crypto currencies with distinct advantages and drawbacks. Bitcoin is obviously the most well-known option, however the 1 BTC is worth thousands of dollars in the majority of physical currencies. This makes it challenging to enter the market without mining to earn money or even having financial stability in which you are able to spend an enormous amount of money on an unstable market like cryptocurrency. It is however widely used in a variety of markets and is an excellent investment. All-time highs continue to be frequently being challenged.

Ethereum is the second most sought-after option, being the second largest cryptocurrency market for 2021. Instead of relying on the peer-to peer system of Bitcoin it's the primary platform through which applications can be directly programmed onto blockchains increasing the scope of the market even more. By acquiring an Ethereum wallet it is possible to access the vast world of NFTs as well as the majority of largest, most well-established blockchain-based games are now accessible and along they also open up more investment opportunities.

Other cryptocurrencies, including Solana are also platforms where apps can be integrated directly in the blockchain. In the case of Solana's it's a more recent currency that boasts more speedy transactions and lower cost.

Do I have to buy Cryptocurrency?

There's no doubt that cryptocurrencies are costly, especially that are successful. However, the old saying is: "The best time to begin was yesterday. The next best time to start is right now." (Unknown).

It is possible to purchase cryptocurrency via an exchange for cryptocurrency or payment services is the most convenient and fastest way to start your journey towards investing, but it is not the only choice and has its own challenges, which is why it isn't suited to all. For networks such as Bitcoin or Ethereum it is possible to invest the thousands of dollars that you can get for one coin. Other networks, like Dogecoin which is a cryptocurrency, the exchange rate is typically quite affordable, but it's a highly volatile market , and Dogecoin hasn't exceeded its value, which is $1USD at the time of 2021. However, this could mean that if one was to purchase a huge amount of Dogecoin at only a few cents and decide to cash out once it increased say, 10 times over at a cost of a couple of cents, you'd will still get 10 times the amount of money you put in. In the opposite case when it's purchased for a few cents and continues to fall 10 times, then you might be able to lose only 10% of the amount that you invested. This is the case in all currencies.

A few trusted exchange companies that accept cryptocurrency are Coinbase, Gemini, Binance.US and Kraken. When selecting an exchange service be sure to consider buying and cash advance fees in addition to the location of the exchange, as additional charges could apply to services that are sent outside of their country of origin. For payment options, CashApp, Venmo, and Paypal are all reliable and are able to trade crypto. CashApp is one of the most popular because it provides something known as "Bitcoin Boost" where users earn Bitcoin through the use of their CashApp card to make purchases.

Exchange services for cryptocurrencies are available but not the only method by which one is able to enter the market. Another way of earning cryptocurrency involves investment brokerage. Companies such as

Robinhood offer commission-free services and permit individuals to invest and trade.

Another way that one could purchase crypto at the time of first starting out are through dedicated ATMs, cryptocurrency retail stores (for instance, LibertyX, and CoinMap sell bitcoin) as well as directly through transactions with a individual.

However, it is not required to purchase tokens using real money however, these strategies do need more energy. There are a variety of tasks that could be done make cryptocurrency much like they are with any other job that pays a salary. They are typically all in the digital world, since it is the place where the coins are native. Some examples will be discussed in the following sections: Blockchain mining gaming as well as writing however it is crucial to recognize that these are only some examples, as more jobs are being created which pay in cryptocurrency because of their nature.

The initial example, known as Blockchain mining was described at the beginning of Chapter 1. It's the process whereby someone dedicates their computer to keep and keep up-to-date a copy the blockchain ledger on the certain cryptocurrency. For their service they receive tokens. It is crucial to remember that mining is built on the Proof of Work (PoW) decentralisation system, and as more cryptocurrencies change to more sustainable, alternative methods, mining will disappear which is why it is crucial to do study on the models used by the cryptocurrencies you're investing. In any case, to start blockchain mining, you will typically spend around a couple thousands of dollars on equipment and that's not even including the electricity cost. The performance of the computer is also an important role in the amount of money is made, since the faster computers are more efficient in mining and earn more money than slow or average computers. Like investments are, it's a risk to determine if the value in the coin going be worth the cost in the beginning and to keep it running?

Another type of cryptocurrency-related job is blockchain gaming that will be further discussed within Chapter 8. In the previous chapter, we talked about various games and applications that play with the metaverse and many were integrated on the blockchain, which allows players to earn cryptocurrency through games and/or by selling products on game-specific marketplaces. While the earnings can differ and are very risky, they are an extremely solid and than a good way to enter the crypto trading world.

Additionally, there are positions that have an employer-employee model in the digital age. An example of this is publishing firms that employ writers to crank out pieces on cryptocurrency and pay them in cryptocurrency.

Placing Your First Investment

We will go through a step-by step process to make your first set of crypto-currencies investments that will depend on the cryptos you've chosen to put your money into, the method by which you intend to split your money, as well as the amount of money you're planning to invest all in.

What is the best amount to invest?

The first thing one should determine is the amount of money they're willing to invest in such an unstable market like the one in the world of electronic currency. Because of the highly risk-averse nature of the business and the risk of losing money, you should not invest more than you're willing to lose, and shouldn't rely upon it to support your financial situation or in other ways. Apart from health issues the risk of investing too much in crypto could also affect the judgment of an individual which can cause stress and leading them to sell their shares in the event that they notice a sudden decline in price this is a viable strategy which will be explained later in this chapter, however not when carried out on impulse and not with a thorough analysis.

Many experts follow the five percent rule: not invest more than five percent of an portfolio of investments into crypto. In the end, the choice should be determined by the person's own confidence level. Some young millionaires have achieved this by investing as much as 10 percent of their earnings in spite of the rule of 5. The primary rule of thumb is to not invest money to meet the needs of both the short and long-term.

In the end, if you are using an exchange such as Coinbase is used to purchase cryptocurrency be aware of the charges for exchange that are in addition to the investment you make. Transfer fees, deposits/withdrawal fees trade fees, as well as Escrow fees can all be applicable which is why they should be considered in determining how much you're willing to invest in the exchange service.

Where to Invest?

In general, it's more secure to begin with the most popular cryptocurrency platforms, like Bitcoin or Ethereum as there is more assurance of their continuing growth than fresh emerging altcoins. Although it is risky, purchasing new altcoins that are fresh would give you the chance of entering into a well-known market at a low cost - that "I used to know them before they became well-known" kind of feeling.

For the cryptocurrency part of your portfolio of investments it is crucial not to put all your eggs in the same basket. This means that considering the budget limits you've set for yourself, it's best to spread your investment across a range of different cryptocurrency. This way, it is possible to invest more money in safer investments before investing in a lesser amount you're comfortable losing in more volatile markets making it an investment that will last for a long time.

"Stablecoins" are a good alternative to add for a small amount to portfolio. They are low-value coins which are less volatile than bitcoins or altcoins since the coins are produced and destroyed to maintain it in the same amount. There is some debate about the utility of the coins, especially because they have not demonstrated significant or even any gain in the long run for investors. The most adored stablecoins is Tether that has barely ever crossed one dollar in price.

As with other investment markets the concept of liquidity is a reality and differs for different cryptocurrency. The markets with high caps like BTC and ETH are among the most liquid currencies in cryptocurrency since they are most sought-after and therefore are the most accepted by the majority of companies. This is why it is much easier to locate customers who are willing to trade in physical cash.

The liquidity factor is important when selecting cryptocurrencies to invest in since the coins that have low liquidity are likely to be difficult to remove when they're not working out.

So, how do one allocate their investment budget based on this information? Typically, when first starting out, investors split their funds between BTC and ETH that are the two most significant and well-established cryptocurrencies, and therefore fairly secure long-term bets compared to smaller altcoins. They also are the most liquid cryptos, meaning that they are the most easily redeemed at any time the investor wants to. A typical and easy-to-diversify plan is simple: 50 percent BTC 50% Ethereum that is a totally acceptable option to consider. A common method utilized to construct an investment portfolio in crypto is to separate investments into high-market caps coin (BTC, ETH, etc.), medium-market cap coins (MATIC, BTT, etc.) as well as low-market cap coin (ATLAS, CGG, etc.). High-cap coins should comprise the majority of your portfolio, around 50 to 70 percent, as they carry the most risk-free and the most likely to give long-term gains. Mid-cap coins could be a further 20% to 40 percent of the portfolio as they fluctuate and aren't as established, however, if they succeed they could provide a substantial ROI (Return on investment). The next step is to ensure that low-cap coins do not exceed 10 percent of the portfolio. These coins will likely be frequently changed around as they are more likely to change hands, and are considered more of an "lottery," since, should one of them rise to a certain value potential ROI could be enormous.

The cryptocurrency portfolio, as previously mentioned it doesn't need to be limited to only include utility and payment coins like these. Some of the portfolio could also be occupied by stablecoins, in small quantities to provide liquidity and liquidity as well as NFTs whether on platforms for trading or gaming platforms. For finalization the discussion, asset allocation doesn't have to be unchanged for the duration of time. Based on the way markets change or individual preferences change and the portfolios' members portfolios, as well as the proportions of the budget will be allocated or even the size of the budget itself , can change as the years progress as markets change, and you are more confident in making decisions about the money you have.

Waiting Out VS Conservative Investment

Overall, the trend shows that younger investors tend to select more risky trades, while older investors opt for more prudent ones. According to the way that younger investors perceive it is that they are able to "wait for the market to open," which means they are able to take longer to wait for the cryptocurrencies in which they've invested to appreciate more than the price they paid. People who are older tend to gravitate towards less successful outcomes, choosing crypto markets which are more likely to be able to be redeemed for an increased value selling price in the near term.

It's not only a matter of age, however, and it is an important idea to consider when selecting an investment strategy. You should ask yourself before deciding which cryptocurrency you will use as part of your portfolio: Do you prefer a shorter-term gains which is less volatile or would you rather sit out the market in anticipation of more chance of success? The problem becomes more complex when you realize that waiting for shorter periods of time, up at three to six months result in more loss than waiting for longer periods of time, for instance, about two years (Subburaj 2021).

When is the best time to buy

If you are considering buying your ways into the market of cryptocurrency there are a couple of important things you need to be aware. It is the first thing that must be repeated constantly because of its vitality that the market for cryptocurrency can fluctuate up to 20% in a single day, as they are extremely unpredictable. But, they're also extremely difficult to forecast and even the most skilled investors can't know the ideal moment to invest in the market.

Another method of determining an entry point into the market is using the dollar cost Averaging (DCA) method. The strategy involves investing the money you want to invest in a cryptocurrency , and then dividing it into equal parts. Each fraction is then invested at regular intervals no matter what the exchange price at the time. So, when all is invested, the price which was paid will be an average market price for the time frame and gives investors a little more assurance over the price they are entering. If, for instance, you intend to buy 10 BTC and you want to buy 10 BTC, you could opt to purchase 2 BTC each on Mondays at 8 a.m. of each week for one month. Even though some days you'd be paying more than prior one, it provides some degree of control over the unpredictable fluctuations. If DCA seems familiar, it's because it is based on the same principles in the same way as the SIP (Systematic Investment Plan) commonly employed in the world of investment in addition to cryptocurrency.

The DCA strategy isn't required to be adhered to exactly. As it can be difficult to pay for an investment that is priced at an increased price than the previous week, what people save a certain amount such as 20% of their budgets to add to the days when the market price was reduced or they believe to be one of the best price of the month, thereby increasing the possibility of lowering the cost of the period of investment.

Understanding the cycles of markets can be crucial to knowing the best entry points. In most cases, cryptocurrency markets create bubbles over about a year or so, which see prices increase and later fall until the cycle repeats. Although this isn't an exact calculation but it can be used as a rough reference, and if the market keeps falling after you invest, it could give you a reason to hold off waiting for the next cycle to end. Monitoring these trends on websites that track them like CoinMarketCap as well as Google Finance can provide useful information, but it cannot be used as a definitive forecast of the future.

Cryptocurrency Paysafecards

Each cryptocurrency requires its individual "wallets," information storage centers and they are not able to blend different currencies. If you're carrying bitcoins, then you must have an Bitcoin wallet. If you're carrying Ether that is, then you must also possess the Ethereum wallet. Every wallet has an individual key that is private and public that must be kept private to anyone other than the owner as keys grant accessibility to cryptocurrency inside.

There are wallets that are able to have the distinction of being "hot" as well as "cold," and these are typically used with various goals in the mind. The hot type of wallet that is connected to Internet. Due to this, transactions that are made in crypto can be carried out quickly and effectively, but since the private keys to your wallet is generated over the Internet the kind particular wallet can be more susceptible to hacking, and in this the owner could lose everything. In this class are exchange wallets that are given by a seller , who holds the private key to a buyer who deposit the money into the wallet, and is unable to access it since they don't know the secret key.

Hot wallets usually hold small amount of cash that is manageable and are typically used by people who are involved in a variety of transactions. A few examples of exchange firms which allow hot wallets through their platform include Coinbase as well as Electrum.

Cold wallets are in the opposite direction and serve as the primary storage option for investors. They are safer and more difficult to hack than hot wallets as they are stored in hard disks, on paper, or any other offline method. If you're using paper it is the case that the public and private keys to the wallet could appear on an envelop paper following the purchase of the wallet through an online site. The paper could be stored in a local bank via safe deposit boxes or in safes at the house of the owner. Anything is possible to ensure it is secure and safe, as it's the only method to gain access to the records of the wallet, other than its blockchain. The issue with both hard drives and paper is a simple one but If the storage device is destroyed, the money in the wallet will be also lost. A few examples of trusted cold wallets include Ledger that creates hardware devices and TREZOR that generates keys that are not online.

Other than accounts, a few companies that offer physical coins for the well-known Bitcoin for a fee in order to cover the cost of manufacturing and shipping costs. However, this could be contradictory to the very premise behind cryptocurrency that is designed to remove physical currency.

There are a few methods to provide additional security for the cryptocurrency account. One is to keep your software up-to-date on your PC and, in general, back up the cold bank account. Another method of preventing the hacker is to utilize multi-signature systems for accessing the funds. That means the authorization of a set of individuals is required for any transaction that is made through the wallet. This way, the hacker's controller is not able to take funds.

To transfer funds to the wallet, at each transaction your wallet's ID (address) associated with it needs to enter into a form following which the cash is transferred.

The goal of achieving a certain return on the investment

After you've invested your first money in crypto, you can establish objectives for each and target ROIs that, in the event that the market does reach them the level, you'll be happy making a withdrawal of some of your cryptocurrency. This will help you establish a strategy that will ensure the longevity of your investment, regardless of how the market is performing at the moment that the goal is achieved.

Of obviously, this isn't an established policy. If you're looking to bet more heavily on your investment You can always keep it for many years or until you are ready to cash out, but it does provide a useful guidelines and lets you better monitor your market's trends with more keen eyes in the near future.

In the event that you discover that the value of the coin has actually reached the targeted ROI, the general direction should also be taken into consideration, because the moment you're in a cycle of market's "bubbling" period, in which it's either rising for the last couple of months or declining it is more straightforward to sell the assets.

Cashing Out

Once you've completed your investment and have waited the market for the time you've decided to wait to wait, whether it's one month or five years in the future, you might be looking to transfer your crypto in the physical currency of your country of residency. This could happen due to the fact that your goal ROI has been achieved and you're looking to cash away a part of your capital while you're ahead or as a means of making your losses more clear after you see a steady decline in value.

How do I cash out My Crypto?

It can be used to purchase specific products, based on the vendor. A lot of large corporations are starting to accept currencies such as Bitcoin to purchase goods, however most people feel that it is more satisfying to simply sell crypto as it is more likely to achieve a targeted ROI using physical currency, which is why the value is more secure and more commonly used in the present day.

There are several methods to sell your cryptocurrency. The most straightforward and easiest is via exchange services as well as hot wallets. In exchange services for which you've signed up, there's generally a chance to sell your cash in exchange for it typically with specific transaction charges. To avoid this, take note of how much money you're able to withdraw and whether the cost is worth the cost. If it's not sufficient to warrant the withdrawal then perhaps think about waiting the market for a longer period to earn more money that you are comfortable with or just withdrawing more money from the amount as is.

Peer-to-peer transactions can also facilitate the exchange of physical currency in exchange for cryptocurrency. In this type of transaction it is you that decides the price and conditions of exchange. The return usually is an electronic transfer.

For some of the more popular cryptocurrency, ATMs are now an option to BTC and ETH. They work the same way as ATMs at banks, and are physical devices that need to be in the area of your choice. The transactions made this way are difficult to trace and are able to be paid in cash, however they depend on the location.

HODLers

Many investors follow the "Hold on for Dear Life" strategy, also known as HODLers. They don't withdraw all of the money they invest with the hope that, after a few years it will be an overall upward trend. While this has made several millionaires, it also has demonstrated that millionaires who once had a lot of money lose all their funds in the course of time as well as those who have never made a fortune with crypto, but rather displaying the high percentage of losses from their portfolios of cryptocurrency.

This is a highly risky one. It is suggested that novice investors choose a more secure approach, knowing when they should stop when they're ahead.

Resolving Your Losses

One reason you might decide to sell your cryptocurrency investment is to "crystallize your losses." This is the case when the exchange rate falls to a level that is lower than 60-70 percent losses on the investment (Anuj 2021,). To eliminate the loss, you need selling off the coins before any damage has been caused and then rebuild your portfolio to reflect. It is possible it is often with low-cap coins where you invest since they're the most unstable.

All-Time Highs

Before investing in cryptocurrency, you must be capable of answering the question what makes someone want to buy coins from me when the price of exchange is on a record record high? For some who are looking to invest in cryptocurrency, it is best to wait until crypto prices have been able to fall recently, but are now climbing again, in order to purchase. Others might consider the price to be rising steadily and would like to buy early. Additionally, there are people who might use the methods described in the "When to buy" portion of this chapter. For instance, they might utilize the DCA strategy, in which it is assumed that the price that the coins are worth is not relevant for the day in question or are monitoring the market's cycles. Whatever the case, these are all aspects to consider when deciding on the timing of selling some among your precious metals.

Be Careful with Your Money

The world of investing in cryptocurrency is an extremely steep learning curve. in Chapter 10 you'll discover some of the most common mistakes and misconceptions investors who haven't invested previously may be making.

Chapter 8: Earning Money From Nfts

In further depth on the various investment options as well as the amounts of cash that have been devoted to the same, there are a few things to consider when you are scouring through non-fungible tokens. The issue was briefly discussed in chapter 7 about the possibilities of incorporating NFT investments into your cryptocurrency portfolio. However what are the best ways to do this if you're non-artists? What are the reasons people purchase and sell NFTs in contrast to tangible or commissioned artwork?

What is Digital Image? Its Worth?

Non-fungible tokens may take on various shapes and designs however, at their core they're simply images. What's the reason for the hype? It's true that the benefit for these NFTs is dependent on the viewer, but in this instance, it's more than "beholders." The interest of consumers in the product is what drives its price that it is sold at, result in millions of dollars for artists who create art that they've created famous brands or who make pictures they think people are interested enough to desire the ownership of, for instance, the well-known NFT that was created by CEO Twitter and an image of his first tweet. The NFTs aren't restricted to being 2D neither. Buildings on the Decentraland gaming platform are also, for example, considered NFTs, simply for being a digital asset on this blockchain-programmed dapp. For these buildings, putting them on LAND that is owned by the buyer may boost the value of the land, and thus make the purchase profitable. This is a sign that building is worth it.

They differ from normal physical or commissioned artworks due to the fact that they must be distinct and have authentic ownership. That means, even while technically, an image from an NFT is able to be downloaded onto any computer, using the PC's built-in functions, the identity of the NFT is forever stored on the blockchain system, which is much more difficult to counterfeit. The information that constitutes the asset is stored as metadata. This is the data that is bought and sold by users not the actual image, offering a evidence of ownership that can't be duplicated through making copies or taking screenshots of the art.

The value of the tokens can be measured in part using four factors such as utility the past owners have liquidity, utility, and projected value (Chang 2020). Two main types of utility are games assets such as buildings from Decentraland or tickets, which be used to gain entry to events. Another method by which NFTs could offer utility is through the partnerships between sellers and other businesses, for instance, for instance, to provide discounts to owners of a certain token. In the near future it is expected that NFTs who have discovered ways to work across metaverses between various platforms will rise with a near-instant value.

Past owners impact the worth of a token as well-known brands, famous personalities, and powerful people attract a large amount of interest and a massive audience for the product. Liquidity is the ease that the NFT is traded in secondary market and the greater the liquidity, the more value as people are drawn to the notion that it is easier to sell than other products. In addition, the projected value will increase the current value for the reason that when people are convinced that they can sell it for more than what they would have paid in the near future and are therefore more likely to purchase today.

Buy NFTs

How do I Purchase an NFT

To buy an NFT first, you must find out where they can be located. Because they are tied to blockchain programming typically, they can only be purchased with utility coins or ones which are compatible with platforms for crypto that support blockchain Dapps. The largest market for NFTs is located on the largest utilitarian tokens platform Ethereum that is why it makes use of ETH for sales. Solana is another example of an utility token platform also has the ability to run it's own NFT marketplaces. It is not as well-developed as Ethereum however, it is relatively new and is growing with the addition of more Dapps.

In these apps, there's no single location to locate NFT marketplaces. They are often linked to dapps. This means that you have to visit these platforms, and be able to locate marketplaces for some of them. For blockchain gaming networks it is common to find an NFT marketplace where they are available for purchase. There are additional marketplaces hubs that are for Dapps that could function as an online store in the sense of OpenSea, Rarible, or Foundation which are fantastic sites for purchasing NFTs. Be aware that when you are using the hot wallet of an exchange platform there are charges for withdrawals and transactions that will be charged once you're in the market to purchase.

The best part about the fact that Ethereum established as a central point of entry for tokens that are not fungible is the fact that it is the most seasoned player on the market. The images or assets purchased are able to be used in any location within the Ethereum space, but they can't be utilized on other cryptocurrency platforms.

In addition, it's not always required to purchase NFTs to begin collecting NFTs. Like with cryptocurrency, performing certain tasks will give the user exclusive NFTs which are extremely liquid. For instance, if you provide liquidity to ETH exchange platforms such as

Uniswap the ERC-721 token (LP-NFT) could be awarded as a basic scratch of the basic information regarding the person who is using the service and the liquidity pool and also the amount. The LP-NFT is able to be traded fairly easily to liquidity pools.

When the NFT is purchased and deposited, it is placed in your cryptocurrency wallet and it can be accessed from there.

Finding the right tokens to Purchase

If you are purchasing NFTs to the intention of later selling them or to boost your other investments you own There are certain methods to consider so that you can select the most lucrative ones for the benefit of consumers. It is crucial to keep your final purpose to think about: ultimately earning more through the NFT than the amount you paid. To achieve this, you'll eventually sell it or make an income passively from it.

In the first place, you must purchase something that you enjoy. Since there is no assurance that it will rise over time and at a higher price in the future. As for anything that is decentralized (also known as DeFi markets, which are very volatile and quite unpredictable, you ought to enjoy the process, at a minimum.

Originality is another thing should be a priority. A lot of NFT art works are based on well-known and expensive works that have had success before However, these imitations seldom perform as well. Are you looking for NFTs that stand out and ideas that haven't been tried before will increase the likelihood that it will increase in value and you can predict a possible trend in the art community.

Additionally, looking up sale histories could provide a clue of the changes in worth of the art. If it has a history of selling at a price higher than what it was purchased for, it's likely that this will remain the scenario. But the reverse may happen as it might decrease in value as soon when you purchase it , resulting in the loss of a significant amount. The best way to avoid making certain extent from making purchases that are not wise is setting an amount you can afford to spend. It is the amount that you are at ease paying for an NFT and could lose when you can't sell it for an increase. A NFT decline in value, like this is another reason to buy something that you like personally since you could remain in it for a long time.

So, you've discovered you have found an NFT You like it and consider to be unique and appears to have a positive or neutral history of sale (perhaps you're even the first person to buy it!). There are some guidelines to later examine the NFT to ensure that it's a worthy purchase. The first is to research the artist's name; what is their identity and their public image and any other projects? There are replicas of the most popular NFTs on marketplaces. They are typically taken or saved, and later shared by fraudsters. Researching the originator and the NFT you wish to purchase will alert you that you're buying a duplicate, instead of an original. You can also be able to observe the NFT's position in the world of commerce So, check whether people generally appear to enjoy it, and what its weaknesses are. You can also study the name that is associated to the NFT. For instance, if the NFT is a part of Axie Infinity, you should know the game and be aware of the population of players that it can be sold.

All of the above is true to finding NFTs to price growth and eventually resales. But, what is another option for passive income? It is a result of fees that are associated with using the NFT to enhance the value of another. In the world that is the realm of the metaverse this might mean charging for the privilege of visiting an art museum that is filled with NFTs collected. In blockchain gaming it is possible to apply the same example of purchasing a building NFT and then putting it in Decentraland LAND to increase its value is also applicable.

Selling and reselling NFTs

NFTs can come in the form of any visual asset, no matter if it's 2D or 3D, objectively gorgeous or not and also in the sense of being interesting but not objectively so. This is why anyone regardless of their identity is able to create NFTs but even if someone does not create art, they are able to benefit from the market by reselling ones that were previously bought.

When creating NFTs The creation, minting, as well as publishing process are all crucial to know. The primary sources of revenue that these images generate should be considered as well. If you purchase and then sell NFTs you must be aware of the resale procedure and limitations in relation to their rights to the artwork.

Making Minting, Creating, and Selling Your NFTs Yourself

The first thing to note is that NFTs can be made out of almost anything. They could be real art pieces that be attractive to buyers due to its beauty, originality and wit. Alternatively, they could be photos or screen shots, depicting something extraordinary, bizarre or even nostalgic. An NFT may also come in the form of audio or video file or text, as well as collectibles or other non-digital objects such as real estate. Anything that is truly exclusive (non-fungible) is able to sell as an NFT but when selecting the format, it should be accessible to upload to the marketplace platform. The most important thing is that creativity is the main aspect for marketplaces that are common.

After a format and idea is selected after which the cryptocurrency is constructed then it's the time to get it created, which is to say it moves from a plain document into an NFT. Minting is the process through which the token is put on the blockchain, thereby locking it forever as an NFT in the market. A royalty clause can also be included by the person who owns the file once the NFT is added to the blockchain. This clause provides for resale royalty that can be made passively after successive owners transfer it to.

In order to create your NFT it is necessary to have a cryptocurrency wallet in place that can store the currency you use on any marketplace you choose to offer it. A previous example in the chapter might remember, is OpenSea. There is a one-time cost for minting. After you have signed up with the market you prefer You can mint the coin there. And after providing some details about the item, it's placed on the blockchain and then officially published and minted. But this is not the final part in the procedure. There are fees for gas and transaction costs to cover the energy required for processing for creating the NFT accessible for sale and also deciding whether to allow the sale to occur in the form of an auction or an auction with a first-come first-buy option. Making a sale, gifting NFTs and cancelling listings or bids, and publishing the identical file across different marketplaces will all incur additional fuel costs and that's the reason it is essential to consider the risks of publishing the information. It is important to determine if the procedure is worth the price.

A lot of talented artists, as well as NFT creators avoid the market altogether and set up their own site and sell their tokens through a primary market that is between the buyers and creators.

After the minting process has been completed when the NFT is published online and accessible by anyone, and can be sold to anyone who is interested.

Ownership Restrictions

To comprehend what exactly it is you own when you purchase an NFT it is important to understand the changes that are taking place on the blockchain. For refreshment of your memories metadata for an asset is saved on the blockchain and the metadata includes all information related to that asset. It's also what's being sold and bought, instead of, say an image. This data that is transferred around is called"token," which is a "token," which clarifies the meaning of NFT as it is "non-fungible," completely unique and is not exchangeable to other types of assets. This "token" metadata proves ownership to the blockchain of the particular asset being offered for sale. Since the only thing being traded is the token for the asset the buyer is given access to a small portion of the digital record and the original asset still the property of the creator.

First, the token can't be duplicated. This preserves the authenticity and uniqueness of the NFT which gives the chance to grow or decrease in value. If there's an online duplicate it is likely to be a scam.

Other rules pertaining specifically to NFTs are set out in smart contracts that outline the terms and conditions that are set in the creation of. They are essentially licenses, and depend on the creator and the token being used. They will indicate the instances where the NFT is freely available as well as those that it is not.

The principal rights granted to the buyer include possession of the NFT through physical or digital transfer and accessibility to

NFT sources file and the right to sell the NFT and to keep a part of deposit.

However in the case of the creator of the original file the Intellectual property rights must be protected which makes copyright theft illegal. This means that new purchasers are not able to provide the NFT accessible to all and can't modify the file or asset or modify it in any manner. Buyers are also not able to be able to sue anyone for the NFT. Of course all of these aspects should be covered within the conditions and terms prior to purchasing the token.

Resale of NFTs purchased

In accordance with the ownership rights of an NFT purchaser the buyer is able to sell the token. This transfer of all the data of the initial asset even though the original asset is protected by the copyright rights of the original creator. In this manner, even though every sale and resale of the NFT are recorded on the blockchain and the price for which they sold are forever etched into the blockchain.

In order to sell an NFT the token can be taken out of your cryptocurrency wallet, and then placed on marketplaces, the same way as any other currency, brand new or not. In this instance it will be classified as an intermediary market.

In most cases when selling an NFT most of the price is paid to you and the seller. Royalties are added to that price which are paid to the creator of the asset, which makes it an income stream for them.

Receiving tokens from gaming

Utilizing non-fungible currency in games that use blockchain is thought by many to not just be their future, but also the future of gaming as well as of technology in general. These projects are among the most complex and therefore challenging, as there's more than just the art that goes into creating NFTs. They must be practical within the game. NFTs have been used into games such as Axie Infinity or Space Atlas where markets and economies are established.

The most interesting aspect of NFTs within games is the fact that it's not necessary to purchase them prior to having to sell them in the future. In the game Space Atlas, NFTs can be found and found throughout the world.

The players who discover them acquire ownership just for picking them up. They can then sell them at their choice, much like the other NFT or other marketplace. In a lesser degree the game Axie Infinity can do the same in that, although one could purchase the NFT or an axie the axie could be created by the player to make new axies owned by them and are able to be sold as own assets.

Chapter 9: Investing In Metaverse

Opportunities

One of the most promising opportunities to earn money through cryptocurrency investments is via the metaverse. This chapter you'll learn the most effective strategies to earn money through blockchain gaming and investments in augmented reality , and all other aspects of the "metaverse." In the beginning, you will be taught how to determine the areas you want to invest, and how to distribute these investments wisely across different platforms , but also across different NFTs as well as other resources on the platform.

Earning Money from Gaming

Blockchain gaming is a major contribution to the coming metaverse, and is one of the biggest industries in the present state of the technology. It is based on a variety of elements that are the dream of the future metaverse like games-specific decentralized economies, which can include an element of interoperability and, most importantly, a connection with NFTs.

To earn profits from games that are blockchain-based as well as the way in how their economies operate need to be analyzed. Even though they operate on a crypto platform that makes use of a particular kind of currency, for instance, Ethereum using Ethereum, these games introduce a new layer of complexity and include their own currencies in game like MANA for Decentraland and SAND for The Sandbox. The distinction between these cashes in games and their parent currencies will be explored.

Play-To-Earn

The idea that of "play-to-earn" will be one which is likely to be mentioned frequently when studying the process of earning money from blockchain gaming. The games that use this idea to motivate players to return. What does play-to-earn mean? It is the centralization of a game as well as the trading of its assets and its identity that leads to the creation of fully-fledged economic systems that allow players earns rewards upon accomplishment of tasks in the game that are then able to be lent to actual cryptocurrency or be traded for it. This can be done since every reward earned during playing has the right to be passed to the participant as part as an NFT.

NFTs

In the majority of blockchain-based play-to-earn-games rewards are in forms of NFTs, rather than directly to cryptocurrency. This gives the user more flexibility as they are able to go and sell the NFT anyplace they wish and at their own price and conditions regardless of whether the marketplace is linked to the gaming platform or not.

Finding or buying the appropriate NFTs is dependent on the specific game. Certain games, such as Axie Infinity, require a understanding of the various characteristics of an axie and how the offspring of breeding perform on the market in the event that selling axies is the objective. In a game such as Decentraland it is the aim to be to build the land NFT you purchase alongside other NFTs like buildings, to improve its value for resale, renting out the space as a landlord, or charge visitors a fee interested in visiting. In addition, you will need be aware of what NFTs will boost your value for the land however, at a more fundamental level, you must think about your location for the land you're buying. Areas that are crowded like those located in the center of cities are more costly for smaller plots since they're more desirable.

It is possible to conclude the fact that there exist a number of ways to acquire NFTs from the game. One is evidently buying them from the game's marketplace. There are times when certain aspects of the game may be bought from other sources like the sale of games' gamer tags in Decentraland through OpenSea. Other game components that can be purchased through a game's marketplace are avatars and props, buildings clothes, items that are available, as well as RPG weapons.

Another method of obtaining NFTs in gaming is to explore and foraging. For instance, in Space Atlas, for example the world is explored and some items are discovered, where the ownership of NFTs is handed over to the gamer. They can then be offered for sale via marketplaces.

Other methods by which NFTs and cryptocurrency could be obtained will depend on the game in question. For instance In Axie Infinity, the player fights in PvE and PvP in order to earn rewards, but also can cultivate potions and items that are also able to be sold to purchase cryptocurrency.

Utility and Governance Tokens

It is well-known in the present that cryptocurrency technology comes with the common name of Bitcoin or Ethereum and the name of their coins that in the context in this case could be Bitcoins (BTC) and the ether (ETH). But, in addition to coins, cryptocurrency also makes use of tokens that are part of the coin itself and can be utilized in the same manner, with but the distinction is that the token is more specific to usage within the specific platform. For instance, Ethereum, which calls its various tokens in the umbrella term "ERC20," hosts ATLAS tokens that are part of the Star Atlas game Star Atlas. The tokens are designed specifically for in-game purchases however they are not able to be used for anything other than the game until transformed into ETH. Another type of token is NFTs. These are tokens that are specially made to appeal to the public because to their uniqueness, but also in terms of entertainment, and possibly aesthetic value. With these two examples it is clear that there are many different kinds of tokens and they can be classified.

There are numerous types of tokens, two of the most common types that are used in gaming are governance and utility kinds. Utility tokens such as ATLAS are created for future usage. It is the most popular in-game currency. This is the instance in the case of ATLAS within Star Atlas. Utility tokens cannot be utilized as investment tokens to earn ROI, so their value doesn't go beyond the purpose for which they are programmed.

Governance tokens, like POLIS of Star Atlas, are a slightly different. Instead of having a future use , at which point they are able to be used and voted on, they are able to vote to vote on game updates and improvements they were created with the intention of keeping games decentralized with distinct developers and creators. With the help of tokens for governance, game plans are able to be voted on or even formulated. These tokens also provide more than cast vote power. In the first place, they could be used to purchase stakes which means a fixed interest rate is set on the tokens, and placed to rest for two years before returning them with the interest accrued. The cryptocurrency over time can be utilized for support the game that is played on blockchain. Another method they could be used is to aid in creating loans, and for yield farming in which cryptocurrency is put into use in order to produce more cryptocurrency. Yield farming is like staking crypto however, it is dependent on liquidity pools.

Making an investment in a game

To begin investing in a cryptocurrency game generally, the game will come with several of its native tokens available for purchase. AXS is in Axie Infinity as well as SAND within The Sandbox, for example. These tokens can be purchased from various exchange companies. It is important to remember that they are the exchanges on which you will keep hot wallets, trade and withdraw money in exchange to various cryptocurrency.

The right game to play where you can invest your money is based on two primary factors: risk tolerance and pleasure. The first is the risk you are willing to allow an investment. For established, well-known games such as Axie Infinity or Decentraland, there is a very low risk which means that even though ROI could be lower than games with higher risk however, they are a better option. However, this doesn't mean that the safer games will automatically provide you with huge returns, but it's more likely. Some games that are less well-known are more risky slmilar to how cryptocurrency coin investments operate high risk has the potential to yield high returns or a huge loss. One example of a brand new game that's high-risk but is likely to see a surge in the market could be Star Atlas. Star Atlas, a game developed using the Solana blockchain, is slated to be among the very first AAA crypto games, which means excellent graphics and an open world. It also means it is developing for a considerable time. To ensure that it is kept in the forefront and build its worth as well as the worth of its tokens, it is released in phases, so players are able to join the game right now if desired, and there's already a community of players despite the limitations of the game.

The other factor upon the basis of which a game's choice on is the pleasure. The primary goal of any game on video is simply entertainment for its players. Although these games are play-to-earn that is mostly tied to their popularity but you should avoid playing a video game that you don't like at all because over the long term you'll be playing the game if you continue to invest money into it.

The end result is that, as with direct cryptocurrencies you're not going to pick only one game token or one game on blockchain where you can invest. Instead, from the section of your portfolio of cryptocurrency, that you have created in Chapter 7 which you may have devoted to blockchain-related games, you can create an entirely new gaming portfolio in which you can divide your investments across a variety of gaming tokens. This manner, you'll divide your investments between more secure tokens as well as riskier ones as well as explore other games that appeal to you.

How to invest in Augmented Reality?

Since the majority of companies that use augmented reality aren't currently heavily involved in the crypto aspect that is the Metaverse we'll look at stock options and strategies related with AR technology. We've talked about the cryptocurrency portfolio and the percentage of your overall investment portfolio you should have in Chapter 7. Stock investments comprise the portion of the portfolio that is likely to yield some of the best returns if appropriately allocated, and in particular this moment, with the metaverse taking off and a huge opportunity to join the metaverse.

When creating an portfolio of investments typically, there are several principal categories: stocks and bonds, mutual funds real estate, and crypto. The most unstable market, should be advised to be used only as a small portion of your portfolio, which is around 5 percent or less. Stocks are the second most risky market, either in a position to yield high returns or risking the entire amount you've invested in it. The risk profile, which is the amount of willingness you have to take a risk with your money and determines what percentage of your portfolio is invested in stocks. This happens typically in conjunction with bonds. 20 percent is typically considered moderate risk, and anything up to 80% can be thought to be high risk and an aggressive one. Bonds are a stabilizing factor to the risk associated with crypto and stocks, which helps to stabilize an investment portfolio's worth that's why, should one make a very little money into stocks, they'd probably increase their investments in bonds and vice versa.

General trends suggest the more cautious investing habits of older individuals, since they are unable to stay out of the market for as long as younger investors who might be saving to retire. This is why we are in the midst of having a time-horizon. Before deciding on which investment options to make and the risks associated with the different stocks, companies or bonds, you must choose your time horizon exactly like you did when deciding which cryptocurrency are worth investing in. If you have shorter time horizons then a low-risk portfolio is the best choice, but If you have a bigger time horizon, you could look into if you feel comfortable with a more volatile but sensible portfolio.

Augmented Reality Stocks

AR as well as VR stocks are still relatively new they were introduced over the last 10 years or around. In that time they've generated billions of dollars, and are on rising with the sudden increase in the popularization of metaverse following of Facebook's change of branding to Meta. Stock options that are safer for AR and metaverse businesses are usually the most lucrative that include Meta, Alphabet (Google's parent company) or Apple. Each of these companies is making strides towards VR, such as meta's purchase of Oculus VR or AR similar to Google's ARCore and Apple's Apple Glasses. The most risky stocks are those for new ventures, possibly developed by smaller companies and less well-known, however basing their decisions on trends in the market and how the world is evolving and consumer enthusiasm, and even your personal belief in the product. You might find an excellent ROI potential.

Chapter 10: The Metaverse Metaverse

How can we define Metaverse? The Metaverse can be broadly described as a blend of digital and physical space. It's a shared, immersive experience, and is the next stage of internet. When we consider web 1.0 which was the time when the internet first began in the early days, it linked us to information. Later, with web 2.0 it was able to connect us to social media. Today, we are connected to people and information through web 3.0 that is only beginning. The internet connects us to information, people objects, and places.

The term"metaverse" was first utilized in the 1990s. Dystopian novel in which people are fleeing from the shattered real world for a completely in a virtual world. If you see the metaverse as a way to solve to the problem, it's just technology getting up to speed with the way we live today. We're all connected to the virtual digital space and can access them via computers or phones. The Metaverse is merely removing the requirement for that small screen.

If you are looking for some pop-culture references for your next reference, the Oasis from the show ready player one can be a good example for a completely connected and holistic metaverse, even though it was depicted as a dystopian universe. We will be using the example of the ready player as we'll return to it in the future.

For Etymologists who study the early Greek, "Meta" means "beyond or after a universe beyond the worlds." It is a prefix that self-references, and for instance, metadata is data that is about data. It is a prefix in Hebrew, Meta translates to is dead. Metaverse technology is several areas however at a higher degree, it's Augmented mixed and virtual reality that you feel using headsets.

Metaverse technology encompasses the internet, and requires an explanation right now. It also encompasses sensors, devices and blockchains linked to it. Blockchain technologies encompass items like cryptocurrency, bitcoin, ethereum, as well as the nfts.

The Metaverse includes 5g machine learning, artificial intelligence Edge computing. This means that it's a variety of different things all rolled into one. From a grander perspective the Metaverse isn't yet here however, the components are in the process of being constructed and the whole thing isn't connected yet. The various technologies must connect in order for this to occur and this will take time.

You can explore a small portion of the Metaverse by visiting areas like decentraland, Oculus apps, ALT Space VR Roblox, Fortnite, and Horizon workrooms. They're not completely formed metaverses, but just fragments of one.

Why should we be concerned over the Metaverse?

In the event that Metaverse isn't fully established yet So why do we need to be concerned? Without getting too dramatic, it's because the transition from the Social Web 2 to a metaverse Web 3 will change everything but maybe not all of it. It will alter the way people consume content, conduct business, shop, the way people communicate with their brands how we get an education, the meaning of art, the way we purchase art, how we interact with each other, and how we interact. In fact, every aspect of your daily life that the internet has a hand in will change.

If you know the impact of change is coming and the changes that are likely to occur it is possible to prepare for it, and be ahead of your competition in the business world or profit from it when you're an business owner. When people think of Metaverse typically, they think of Augmented and Virtual Reality first. That's AR and VR. This is a good thing.

Augmented as well as Virtual virtual reality headsets have been, and will remain the main way we access the Metaverse. Today, we can connect to the Metaverse using a mobile phone but in the near future I'm thinking that phones will move from being in a pockets or in the palm to being on our faces.

Some of the most notable pioneers in headsets or smart glasses creation include Facebook with its Oculus quest 2, Microsoft with the Hololens 2, and Magic Leap that recently announced the launch of its Magic Leap 2. We will likely be seeing headsets made by Apple and Google in the near future, too.

In relation to Facebook you might have been informed about the fact that Facebook altered its brand name and changed it to meta. Based on Mark Zuckerberg, they rebranded to be more in line with their new vision of developing technology that allows you to appear as a person in a virtual space or even appear in real-world spaces as a hologram wherever on earth.

According to the New York Times, Facebook already has more than 10,000 people working in its labs that are working with Augmented and Virtual reality projects to the sake of scale. It's about twice the amount of people on Twitter's entire team and by 2021 Facebook has already spent approximately 10 billion dollars in metaverse-related investments.

According to the Times, Zuckerberg and the Facebook team are likely to take action to tackle four of the major issues that are affecting Facebook. These include:

App abandonment: Younger users are leaving Facebook and Instagram in favor of more modern platforms such as TikTok.

The Platform Risk: Facebook mobile runs on Android and iOS. Two platforms Facebook does not control.

Risks to Regulatory Compliance: As you may have read in the news , reputational risk is a constant issue for the company. We will not go into any specifics about Facebook and its rebranding.

Metaverse experts are worried that having one company like Facebook have control over the Metaverse could cause a dystopian scenario similar to the ones by the film Ready Player One. One company controlling the Metaverse could mean that they have access to huge amounts of personal information gathered when traversing the digital world and could have disastrous consequences. There is a suggestion that the Metaverse could be open , meaning that no single company or corporation has control over the entire thing, but this will be more difficult to implement logistically.

Monetizing the Metaverse

One of the most important issues we have yet to address in The Metaverse concerns how individuals or companies will earn money in the Metaverse. This has led to Facebook many legal issues, as it has because of web 2.0. As of now, Facebook, like most Web 2 platforms, relies on advertising to generate revenue. These platforms, such as Youtube, Facebook, Tick-tock and Instagram are accessible for free. These companies earn profits to pay for their services by showing ads.

A lot of people don't like the thought that they live in an online reality that is where the vast majority of your point of vision is filled with adverts as well as product positioning. We don't know the answer for this yet however, I think the business model in Ready Player one The novel, and not even the film is genius. Instead of ads, when you pay for access to the other worlds of the Metaverse. However, you could travel anywhere without cost, and it took longer. That's how Oasis generated enough money to support its own operations, primarily through the cost of a bus. It was possible to access vital services like education, access to information and services for no cost, just like we have access to the internet today. This is how Oasis earned money to support itself.

Cryptocurrencies use a similar system. When you buy crypto, it is moved from one location to the next and must pay a fee for gas to transfer the assets and confirm your ownership through the blockchain. It would be fascinating to find out if the can apply the same idea in the monetization of the Metaverse, so that we do not have to live in a world that is packed with advertisements.

Is The Metaverse a Good Choice for Everyone?

You might be wondering if it's possible to not be a part of the Metaverse. You can stay out of the Metaverse the way you are able to stay away from the internet currently. It's possiblethat millions of people don't have internet access that is reliable but not out of necessity. If you're in a position to choose whether to use it in any way, or otherwise, you may decide not to participate in commerce or engage in social interaction in the metaverse. However, I believe that most people will, particularly younger generations.

Gaming

Generation Y has realized that video games such as roadblocks aren't only in the realm of mindless gaming however, they're also an opportunity to socialize and make connections with others and the Metaverse is going to become that way, but on an enormous scale.

Technologies to support the Metaverse

We have talked about the future of technologies, but what about technology that is in Metaverse is likely to render obsolete. I would expect for a slow shift from smartphones to wearables such as smart glasses. There will be people who will always depend on their smartphones in the similar way that some households have landlines but the majority of people will switch towards wearables. The reason for this isn't only about the latest and most advanced technology. There's only so much tech you can pack into a smartphone.

As for me, my iPhone has around five cameras and it's at its limits. My Oculus comes with four cameras, but they're only beginning to get established. However I'm not sure we'll be walking around with an Oculus-like device in our hands. The actual appearance as well as aesthetics that are associated with the Oculus are an extended way to be taken. I'm sure there'll be something that's simpler, less bulky looking, and similar to an ordinary pair of glasses. We're still a long way from that, however there's an incredible quantity of power that's packed into the Oculus.

Creators from the Metaverse

If you're a writer or aspiring to be a creator You may be thinking how you can utilize metaverse technology to benefit yourself. It's amazing because the Metaverse can allow you to reach levels of creativity that weren't possible previously. It is because you have the ability to accomplish what is impossible in the metaverse. You can show your appearance however you'd like. In the Metaverse your body is represented as an avatar.

Today, Avatars appear to be pretty standard and cartoon-like or animated, however several companies are currently working on more realistic avatars. With these Avatars you can personalize your avatar to be shorter, taller and possess purple hair, not have hair or skin color, are skinless, possess pegasus wings, appear to be burning and have tattoos that change according to your heartbeat and mood This is your Avatar and it's all just you.

NFTs

Digital art is something can be collected and displayed on the metaverse. It may be a digital rendering of a 3D-animated mural or an exclusive collectible. It's possible that the Facebook connect keynote offers an idea examples of these that are an original piece of 3D moving street art, but that's only the beginning. Certain major players as well as scrappy startups are working to build the Metaverse and should you want to know more about the ways you can invest in these businesses I've already covered the subject in my book. However, before you invest in these businesses, first and foremost, there are three game engine platforms that drive the Metaverse. They include Unity 3d, Unreal and Epic games. They are huge players in the project space.

As we've mentioned in the past, we have Facebook who is aiming to be the platform upon which all metaverse universes are constructed as well as the integrator of all experiences. There are cloud computing providers like Amazon web services, also known as AWS, Google Cloud, Microsoft Azure. Cloud computing is expected to play a major role and will be a key element in building the Metaverse. There are many other businesses creating applications and experiences that are built on top of these fundamental infrastructure level businesses.

Businesses in the Metaverse

If you're an enterprise or are aspiring to become a business owner The Metaverse is going to present an entirely new set of problems. The most significant difference that can take an extended time to grasp and understand is how to implement the concept about digital property to your business and the products and services you provide. People who were raised with the internet are able to recognize digital ownership, which proves that you have the physical asset.

What distinguishes the Metaverse unique is the fact the fact that they are integrated into the blockchain to make NFTs which are non-fungible currencies. We now have digital assets that are unique and are able to move between platforms. If you're a company owner or creator of content it could raise some warnings regarding your long-term strategy. Digital assets may create a new revenue stream dependent on the product you are selling.

Chapter 11: What Facebook Integrates With

The Metaverse

This section will explore how Facebook is now meta and is integrated into the Metaverse and how they play a role in the NFTs, also known as non-fungible tokens.

Mark Zuckerberg recently announced that Facebook changed its name to meta. This change is meant to help the company achieve its goal to become the most prominent metaverse-focused company. So, what is it that on Earth is that? The Metaverse is described as the next evolution of internet technology. We are living in web 2.0 in the present. We are starting to move to web 3, which involves the introduction of immersive technologies such as Augmented as well as Virtual reality, blockchain technologies like NFTs and cryptocurrency.

NFTs are digital assets that's ownership is secured by the blockchain, typically the Ethereum. Zuckerberg as well as Facebook and the Facebook team have made it open about their plans to become the metaverse platform, with huge implications regarding the future of nfts in the event that Facebook slash meta proves successful. Michelle Shaw, the head of metaverse-related products at Facebook stated that they would like to facilitate the ability of users to sell NFTs and entrepreneurs to create companies that operate in the Metaverse.

One of the most important questions concerns whether Facebook metaverse will be as open as decentraland or will be closed, meaning it is necessary to be in the Facebook ecosystem to be able to work on it. They have a virtual currency that is now known as Diem which was previously called Libra. Following Facebook Connect's keynote Facebook connection keynote I'd like to spotlight five markets within Facebook's Metaverse in which NFTs are expected to play a significant part. They include:

avatars, and gear For Avatars: Zuckerberg drove home the idea that the Metaverse is a way to connect people. In contrast to our present web 2.0 configuration Connecting digitally means that every body appears and not just floating head on an LCD screen. To represent yourself visually within three dimensions you require avatars. Avatars are live-time scans that show your body and face as well as like cartoons or animated. They can be incredibly realistic or totally unbelievable. It's not easy to imagine an avatar even though you're a digital asset which can be purchased and traded.

I believe there's an immense market opportunity for any company that is able to discover a way to create real-looking NFT avatars of an individual at a specific date and time. I believe there's an enormous intellectual property war that is on the Horizon with regards to Avatars and I'd like an entrepreneurial company to be the one to end the issue.

Digital Clothing Digital Clothing NFT market for fashion-related NFTs all over the world is expected to grow massively. We're already witnessing that through companies like Dress X, designer brands which are already embracing the industry, even though there's no place in the Metaverse currently in which you can wear designer digital equipment. Zuckerberg made a reference in his speech that the design of the virtual world could be something that users can purchase, keep and sell.

Virtual Spaces are also known as Nfts in the main event they all get together in a floating cube. This kind of NFT is especially appealing since they permit shared experiences. It's not like the artwork of a painting or a card which sits on a shelf. It can be a space to meet and interact with other people.

Events are a bit different from the spaces. In the case of concerts, musicians can offer NFT tokens that allow the audience to go from the live concert as a virtual one or even the live concert on digital hologram. It could be a meetup or a virtual after-party an AMA, and so on. This arrangement could also be used in conjunction with sporting events, such as the Super Bowl.

Creative Content Creators are able to make use of NFTs to reach their fans and increase their business. In the world of the creator economy, I've seen digital art tokenized being distributed to fans, and tokens used to support the creator, granting the fans access to events that are limited and the first content releases, such as videos or music. In the context of the creator economy and NFTs, it's a mix of the various categories I've mentioned previously, but targeted at content creators.

Gaming: There's significant importance of NFTs in games for gaming and the gaming sector's long-term future. In his keynote speech, Zuckerberg announced that a version of GTA will be accessible through the quest. This is massive too. He didn't mention if there will be NFT items that are available within the game however GTA is a perfect example of a game that can explode if tokenized game items are included.

These are only the top five sectors in which I can see meta having an impact on NFTs. In that sense, we're very early on the journey to NFTs along with the Metaverse. It's anywhere from five to ten years from widespread adoption. the main items that need to be done prior to that:

We require a headset that can be worn comfortably by people for prolonged periods of between 8 and 12 hours.

We have to establish the infrastructure, and then connect metaverse applications.

At present, we're dealing with isolated metaverses, like decentraland roadblocks as well as the Sandbox. Each one can be visited in isolation, but you aren't able to travel between them and that type of connectivity must occur in a large scale. The individual applications help to increase adoption and get people acquainted with the intricacies and the culture of the Metaverse. They also teach how to utilize NFTs.

Chapter 12: Metaverse Technology

Concerning Health

This section will explore the ways that people have utilized the Metaverse to improve their health and alter how their brains work to allow them to achieve incredible things. This may be a shock to you, as the latest news regarding Metaverse is about becoming brainless drones. Though that's certainly a possibility I thought it would be interesting to explore the positive aspects of the metaverse.

We will be looking at the research-based, measurable effects that occur to people who are in the Metaverse, and how these outcomes can be replicated either at home or in a clinic setting. This book is a mixture of 95% science and 5% my personal opinion and speculation.

What exactly we mean by the term "Metaverse? It is the Metaverse is a broad term used for the merging of digital and real space. It includes mixed reality and Virtual

Reality. The majority of people connect to the Metaverse using phones however, we'll eventually make use of a headset of a type, possibly a slimmer version of Oculus Magic leap, and Hololens.

As an architect, I'm spending much of my time in the headset or in on a computer and at some point I began to think what kind of excessive screen time could be harmful for me. I'm a victim of a genetic mutation which makes me susceptible to macular degeneration. I'm naturally concerned about my eyes health. I've wondered whether the awe-inspiring, highly detailed and rich virtual environments could influence or alter the way in which my brain develops neural connections. It could also reduce my already slender attention duration.

It is evident that a lot of people, including parents and neuroscientists, have wondered the same thing. And the first findings are shocking. A few of the most common negative side effects of living in the metaverse include motion sickness, which you might have already heard about and eye strain as well as more serious issues like seizures and persistent short-sightedness, also known as myopia. It's not even considering the mental health issues that come with from spending long periods of time in a world where every person can be a perfect avatar but there are some positives and that's the point of this article is about.

The research has shown that, even though the current Virtual as well as Augmented simulations aren't super-realistic however, they're realistic enough to allow you to make neural connections even after entering VR. This process of rewiring is known as neural plasticity.

Neuroplasticity is a subject of intense research and something that you can test through brain scans. It's a skill you can use throughout your existence. Your brain is constantly creating new connections among brain cells as well as making sure you're using them every day. In turn, it is also cutting connections aren't used often.

Neuroplasticity is a factor when you hurt your body or brain. For instance, if you injure your knee's skin or suffered a stroke which damaged the part of the motor cortex the brain that regulates your leg. After the injury, you might experience muscles weakness, or perhaps your leg is totally disabled.

If you're recuperating from a medical condition, your doctor may refer the patient to physical therapy which is where you'll be working out in the gym for physical therapy to aid in regaining the muscle's strength. If you've suffered stroke, you'll also need to teach your brain to develop new neurons in the affected region so that you can gain control over your leg. Anyone who has gone in physical therapy even for minor accidents will be able to tell you that it's extremely difficult, tedious and even demoralizing.

There is a growing body evidence suggesting that if you put people into the VR experience and then allow them to perform the same exercises in a practical way but with a more meaningful immersive experience, you can put them into a video game which is also physical therapy.

They will heal themselves faster and with greater efficiency. After the VR experience, the brain will create neurons in the area of injury and will allow the patient to be more mobile and walk around again, or gain the strength. A few companies are that are using Augmented as well as Virtual reality to trick your brain into starting the process of neural plasticity and forming more neural connections in the present.

One of these companies is a Texas-based startup known as Neuro-Rehab VR Full Disclosure. After I learned that this was actually real and backed by neuroscience, I was excited to begin working with this company. They've set up VR virtual reality simulations of physical therapy at clinics and hospitals across the US. It's exciting to witness a company making a difference in lives through VR. They are currently working on an VR application that you can utilize at home. If you require physical therapy or rehabilitation from a sporting injury the app will be easily accessible.

There are many other companies making use of the Metaverse to enhance your brain's performance. Some that I like are helium that has an app that is immersive that helps you to meditate and help your brain remain in a state of meditative for longer.

Fundamental VR is the Augmented and Virtual Reality application to train surgeons to perform complex surgeries and procedures. There is already muscle memory in them and know-how when they are undergoing an operation for the first . Another option I'll mention is Oxford VR, which assists patients in overcoming anxiety and fears for just two hours. It's amazing.

Reaching the extremes that lie beyond VR as well as neuroscience sort of been my most recent fascination or at least the basis of my current fascination, and it's an area I'm watching closely and would like to get involved in.

What we're saying is the potential for metaverse technology such as Augmented Mixed and Virtual Reality to alter thoughts or habits and aid people in reaching their goals more quickly. This is basically personal growth on demand and, with the neuroplasticity process, your goals do not necessarily have to be physical or the same as those we encounter when we talk about neuro rehab. The researchers are also discussing helping people to change their brains so that they can achieve their dream jobs and find a love partner and start a company. gain wealth, reach financial independence, and lose weight. These are the kinds of things that the self-help market has produced billions of dollars by trying to market.

Let's examine what scientists have to say and currently neuroscience research suggests that this is likely to occur. Research is showing that mastermeditators can concentrate on a specific state in which they generate brain waves that change their neural circuitry through the combination of thoughts and emotion. There is no way to assist the meditators with using a scalpel and electrode. They're all doing this inside their brains which is incredible.

If you've thought of"the law of manifestation" or "law of attraction," that's what these practices are seeking to harness and accomplish. But, I think they're often not actually being able do this, and the reason is that these kinds of practices on by themselves aren't sufficient to cause the chemical or physical changes within the brain. If there's an alternative to purchase an 29.99 VR application available on the app store, it will trigger the emotion and brainwave pattern you can use every day to enhance your thoughts and help you to act in a manner that you'll achieve great success in doing this.

It's easier rather than spending 10+ years studying the techniques to be a master meditation. It's possible, and extremely amazing. If you're looking to recreate this experience at home, merely stepping into the VR simulation of a mansion located in Los Angeles' Hollywood hills will appear as the house in real life. Technology is wonderful but it's not great. There's of more.

In the beginning of the story I was concerned about the Metaverse could be harmful to my health. It might have been, however it seems like it could be a great benefit for your brain when used correctly. With the way that the Metaverse is likely to overtake our lives although it may appear as a nice to include feature, I believe it's something we should be pushing for inclusion in the core of the Metaverse. If we were to implement the ability to let users be aware that a photo is a photoshop on Instagram right from the beginning and completely alter the user experience of that app.

Chapter 13: What To Earn Money In The

Metaverse

In this part we will look at the various methods to make money in the metaverse. Let's take a quick look back at the Metaverse to see if you've been unable to remember. Metaverse is a virtual world. Metaverse can be described as an internet-connected universe and is a virtual place in which you can live your life in virtual reality. It is accessible via a display similar to your laptop or computer, or by using VR headsets and enter directly into virtual reality.

There is a myriad of things in the Metaverse. You can attend an event, hold an informal meeting and play games with your buddies There are a lot of things. It is an entire virtual world that allows you to make everything. There are many properties within the Metaverse. These include:

Decentraland

Sandbox

Axi infinity

Illuvium

Roblox

The main question is how can you earn profits through the Metaverse? That's the question we're discussing in this segment. Therefore, the most important strategy, and also one of the most obvious aspects of the Metaverse virtual world is the virtual world.

Purchase A Land

It is possible to first purchase property or land in the metaverse, just as I've already explained the steps within this publication. When you purchase your property normally comes with the form of an NFT (Non-fungible currency). The most famous or largest name that exists in the world of purchasing real estate in the Metaverse is decentraland. Decentraland lets you buy land. The website is decentraland.org or utilize Next Earth. Visit the marketplace. Find the most affordable parcel of land at the price in mana. It is the smallest, most affordable piece of land you can purchase from decentraland. One mana currently costs 2.77 cents US for the smallest piece of land available in the Metaverse.

There are many ways to explore the Metaverses and check out what they can provide. You can also visit https://metaverse.properties/, which is the metaverse company, and it is really interesting because they are the first kind of virtual real estate company. When you click REIT which is Real Estate Investment Trust, an entity that was created to purchase real estate and transfer funds into shareholders.

This is an exceptional chance, and they're also claiming to be an REIT that is metaverse. It's true that I've never heard of previously. I buy directly from Metaverse however, you could make a lot of money. They will purchase it from you and hope to sell it at the higher price. It is possible to rent it out, advertise on it, or advertise for an other company, or build your own home on it and perform many various things using it. However, the goal is to purchase it, and earn some money while you wait to sell it at a greater price. Like I said, if you were looking to purchase property in the decentraland region it was necessary to purchase it using mana.

What is mana? Mana is a type of token or coin that is associated to the metaverse decentraland. Every property in the metaverse is going to have its own tokens. In the case of land properties the token is known as mana. If you travel to another metaverse, which is called Sandbox it is the token Sand. For Axia infinity, it's AXS and for Illuvium it's ILV.

If you visit market cap for coins you will see decentraland as well as the token that is that is associated with the Metaverse. To purchase or sell anything similar to land in the Metaverse, you need to utilize mana. If you look at your price of mana every day since

Facebook announced their announcement, it's increased.

Metaverse token

If you do not want to purchase property in the Metaverse then you can purchase the token that is associated with that Metaverse. If you believe that the Metaverse will explode completely and you don't want to purchase property in that Metaverse You can purchase the Metaverse tokens and receive a similar share so long as the Metaverse performs well in the long-term. It's similar to buying stock. Instead, you're purchasing the token or coin related to the Metaverse or to trade on the Metaverse.

Metaverse Index

If you're not looking to purchase individual tokens or coins however, they do offer Metaverse Index. Metaverse index is a repository for a range of metaverse tokens. Here is a listing of all the different tokens contained in the index.

If you purchase an index you're purchasing the whole set of the tokens that are included inside the. If you buy the MVI, which is the metaverse's index ticker symbol MVI you're buying a smaller percentage of all the cryptos that are included in the index.

It's a fantastic chance to invest because instead of picking and choosing the Metaverse you believe will work well, you can invest on the Metaverse index. It offers a wide selection of nearly all coins. According to me, it's a great alternative for those who don't want to go through a whole bunch of coins. This is an excellent alternative.

In the process of creating NFT's

Another method of earning money in the Metaverse is to making NFTs. This is not about the land. We're discussing everything

162

else you can purchase and offer for sale in the world of Metaverse. This includes art, avatars Products, Buildings and Products Wearables and anything else you could design using your computer. Then upload it to the Metaverse.

It is essential to have a basic design abilities. It shouldn't take long to master these skills. Explore platforms such as Skillshare or Udemy to learn these skills, and then upload them onto the Metaverse and then sell them. Another option is to design something custom like avatars for individuals or even custom-designed homes that mimic homes of other people.

Metaverse Stocks

It is possible to invest heavily in this stocks. So I have invested in seven or six stocks, and I am now super positive about Amazon, Microsoft, Facebook and Apple. I am holding each of these four companies.

Metaverse service

You might not like stocks, but you are interested in other services such as creating a business from the metaverse. I would suggest checking the metaverse's services. Many people want to join the Metaverse and get their name well-known within the Metaverse. They'll require some help in this process like making an avatar that appears similar to them, and creating an estate for Paul in the Metaverse with a fancy yacht, or a massive Lamborghini that is parked in front of his house.

Everything has to be created and designed. If you are able to create that, then you can make a company out of it. Then, you can provide your services through platforms such as Fiverr. There are a myriad of ways to earn money. You can also purchase these services, mark them up , and sell them to someone else or learn to make these services yourself and then sell them directly via Fiverr as well as Upwork or other platforms. In any case it's the same idea that people are purchasing avatars and skins, nfts, shoes and Gucci flip-flops to ensure that they appear cool when they walk around in the Metaverse. It's a great possibility for you if you're an artist or you're able to master basic design techniques.

I believe there's a huge opportunity to profit from this as you can offer the services via platforms like Fiverr and similar to Upwork.

Chapter 14: Etfs, Stocks, And Stocks

Recently, Mark Zuckerberg announced that Facebook changed the name of its company to Meta platforms. The ticker symbol would change to MRVS on the 1st of December. He released a short video about how he sees the Metaverse and the ways in which Augmented as well as Virtual reality will transform the way we perceive our digital environment. The Metaverse, as he sees it is the place where the physical world is joined by the digital. In this section we'll talk about the specifics of what this means.

If you think it will occur or not, given that there are 10,000 employees, or 20 percent of Facebook's workforce is engaged in the development of AR as well as VR gadgets, then the truth of it is likely to be realized. Facebook is also believed to have an unlimited amount of funds AMD and is estimated to spend five billion dollars a year on metaverse-related research and development. They also bought Oculus in 2014 for a sum of two billion dollars.

I believe that a version of the Metaverse is likely to be created It's not a question of if the Metaverse will ever be created, but an issue of the time when it will happen. The Metaverse is, as a whole, isn't owned by Facebook however, it is evident that Mark has been trying to claim a piece to it by changing the name of the company's company to Meta.

This is why we'll discuss is the Metaverse is, how it will be like and how you can start early with different ETFs and stocks that may play a significant role in the future Metaverse.

What exactly is the Metaverse? The Metaverse has multiple definitions It could be called the latest big version that is the web. Much like how the mobile web was built upon the conventional internet of the 90s and the early 2000s, the Metaverse is an endless network of interconnected virtual worlds that allow people to interact, play and socialize with VR AR, Augmented Reality, and other gadgets.

Specifications of The Metaverse

No lengths or limits

It is guaranteed that the Metaverse will never go off and inaccessible for updates to the maintenance and server reboots. The users will be able login and out at any time they want without needing to save or load their data. Everybody will be experiencing the Metaverse simultaneously and live simultaneously.

My closest example I could provide to share with you is from the year of 2019. Fortnite had an in-game concert that let you watch DJ marshmallow playing a virtual set. If you were logged into the game at the same moment, the whole game that was being played at the time would be playing the same game. If you're in a voice chat with your fellow players at the same time it's as if you were in a concert. The Metaverse seeks to be akin to the real world, where everything happens in one place and many millions of users will communicate through a physical and digital world.

There will be an economy

With the increasing number of users occupying this digital AR as well as VR, companies as well as individuals will be selling goods and services across the Metaverse. Imagine your favorite brands that sells digital products in the Metaverse. For example, Louis Vuitton might be selling a bag made of digital that your virtual Avatar is able to carry. I'm certain that users will be able to establish their own small enterprises in the Metaverse. For instance an established business that has been launched in nearly every kind of multiplayer online game is typically a player-owned casino. This way, attention can be monetized. The more attention is poured in the realm of the Metaverse there are more chances for transactions to occur.

Unlimitless Potential for UCC

There's boundless potential for user-generated content. Although there will definitely be companies and corporations that create experiences and content in the Metaverse however, individuals can significantly influence the vast majority of the Metaverse's content. The model of user-generated content lets Metaverse to be Metaverse to be extremely adaptable and in line with the most recent trends. In addition, many corporations like Nike as well as

Microsoft have already joined the growing popularity of the Metaverse.

In the late month of the month of October Nike registered seven trademarks at the United States patent office for virtual goods that can be downloaded Retail store services, which include virtual products as well as non-downloadable virtual footwear etc.

It is evident that there has been the institutional adoption of firms that deal in digital goods within the Metaverse and leads us to the next step.

Crosses Physical and Digital Environments

All of it will be compatible and can be used in both physical and digital worlds. Also, Augmented reality and Virtual reality will play a major role in the Metaverse. The first thing

170

that comes to mind this moment is the Amazon AR view. In the Amazon AR perspective, buyers are able to test products at home virtually before they make the purchase. This idea isn't that new however it might be very prevalent in the Metaverse.

Another intriguing aspect is that items can be traded in the Metaverse along with other products that are on the same platform, regardless of brand or community. As an example, imagine an environment where you can trade a good fortnight-long skin with something that is part of your virtual home, as a couch in the digital world. The barriers will all be taken down, which is what the Metaverse is all about.

How to Invest in the Metaverse

After you have learned about the Metaverse How can you invest, as it's in its early days? The Metaverse is likely to be some time away, however, stocks and companies are crucial for its development. We'll start by discussing the potential market as per Bloomberg intelligence. The market for metaverses in the world could grow to 800 billion dollars by 2024.

Market Opportunity: Global Market Size

Bloomberg Intelligence believes the market opportunity for the **Metaverse** can reach **$800 billion by 2024.**

An invest estimates that **revenue from virtual worlds** could approach **$400 billion by 2025** up from the approximate **$180 billion in 2021.**

Virtual Worlds Revenue Growth

It is also possible to add metaverse infrastructure as an potential. Round Hill Investments, a company that invests in round hills, believe that there will be that there will be a 2.5 trillion potential in 2030. For a bit of background, here is the whole energy category with the market capitalization in the range of 2.95 trillion dollars. Likewise, the whole real estate market is worth 1.8 trillion dollars.

There are two major ways to invest in the Metaverse at present. One is to invest in the creation of content as well as the infrastructure part that is part of the Metaverse. If you're looking for an all-encompassing investment in the Metaverse you can invest in an ETF. I've heard that Round Hill Investments offers an ETF known as the meta ETF that is designed to give you exposure to companies active within the Metaverse.

A few of the companies the ETF is investing in include infrastructure firms, such as, Cloudflare and Nvidia, or gaming engines. To create virtual worlds, you can choose between Unity along with Roblox.

If you're looking to invest in the Metaverse, or even the whole it's worth looking at Meta ETF. Their expense ratio however, is very excessive at 0.75 percent. The ETF was introduced in June of this year, we do not know what it will fare with regard to performance. If you're looking to invest in the space. If so, one simple option is to take a look at meta ETF investments and pick companies that can fit in with your overall investment plan and portfolio.

Let's look at two companies that are worth keeping an eye on within the Metaverse.

Matterport

Matterport is a world-class spatial firm that digitalizes reality. Their current focus is recording real estate using cameras and then digitizing the information and transforming it into 3D models. Realtors can then make use of these models and present the models to prospective clients without going into a home.

One of the major problems that the Metaverse will face is the necessity to digitize and transfer every aspect of physical actual world to a digital environment. This is the place Matterport is into the picture, and could become one of the largest participants in the Metaverse within the next 10 years since it dominates the booming market for the 3D digital transformation of the physical world into an electronic world. If a competitor does not come along and is better than Matterport and faster, I don't think Matterport being less important in this endeavor.

Matterport is already a collection that includes 38 patents and 28 patents in the process of being filed, so the newest competitors are likely to have a difficult time getting into the business. Matterport currently earns five-quarters of its revenues via SAAS (subscription as a Service, and one of the main reasons for Matterport is its broad customer base. with less than 10% of the revenue coming from their top customers, and with 250,000 customers in the entire spectrum, Matterport's business isn't heavily influenced by any particular customer.

Matterport currently works with companies such as Redfin, Century 21, Airbnb, Hyatt nationwide, Autodesk and the list continues. One interesting aspect of the recent earnings call on the 3rd of November was that Matterport actually has collaboration in place with Facebook (meta). Matterport is working together with meta AI research to create AI technology for both the digital and physical worlds.

The report's story is a bit uncertain in the light of the valuation of Matterport. With 52 percent price per sale ratio, and market capitalization at 4.9 billion dollars Matterport can be an highly valued business. The 4.9 billion dollars market cap when compared with its revenue for the 12 months trailing it of 100 million dollars is an enormous amount of value for just a few profits.

In one of their Investor calls there's a forecast

Index	-		P/E	
Market Cap	4.83B		Forward	
Income	-		PEG	
Sales	105.09M		P/S	
Book/sh	6.06		P/B	
Cash/sh	0.00		P/C	
Dividend	-		P/FCF	

of an adjustable market of 240 billion dollars. They think they've been able to penetrate around four percent or under four per cent.

Concerning their earnings conference that I mentioned prior, Matterport had slight misses in their EPS and revenue. Due to those earnings, they began trading lower after hours, around 6.6%. Therefore, even though they reported low earnings, if are positive about Matterport for the long-term this could be a good time to invest in.

$240B global TAM opportunity as properties move online...

4B		
Buildings	Matterport Illustrative ARR	
20B	@1%	@5%
Spaces	Penetration	Penetration
@ $1	200M	1B
Per Space / Month	Spaces	Spaces
$240B	$2.4B	$12B
TAM	ARR	ARR

Unity

The next option to consider is Unity. Unity is a software platform that lets developers can make and sell their games on a variety of platforms which include Windows, Android, iOS, Playstation, and more. Around 60 percent of AR and VR games currently developed using the Unity platform. Although the majority of their revenue is from the gaming sector, Unity is expanding into other sectors.

The second quarter in 2021 Unity bought metaverse technologies, which is a 3D optimization software firm. This acquisition will mean that professional developers can quickly and easily bring 3D models into Unity and then optimize their models for development in real-time.

Unity is not without its questions about its profitability and valuation. As the graph illustrates, Unity produces revenue like crazy with an increase year after year to the right.

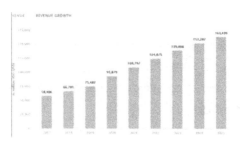

Their gross margins are impressive at about 80 percent, however their operating and net margins are in the red due to R & D costs. They're spending lots of money investing in their own company, which is beneficial, but their financials could look bleak for the foreseeable future. Although they may not turn an income for a long time, Unity has a cash cushion of about 1.6 billion dollars which can be used to offset the costs in the interim.

Concerning the value, the stock has high growth expectations, with the price to sales ratio of 38 enterprise value, 44 for sales. an price per book 21.3. The company is trading a more expensive in comparison to other IT companies. It's currently Unity has been growing in revenue with an annual compounded growth rate of 142% over the last three years, however, analysts anticipate that it will be close to 29.3 percent in the coming 10 years. Given these growth levels, Unity's current price could be justified. The median analyst price ranges from 130 and 116 dollar per share.

The most important thing to note about Unity is that its stock isn't inexpensive. But, its revenue growth rate and massive number of monthly active users across all kinds of Unity apps is 2.7 billion active monthly users. Their continuing momentum and other industries may justify a higher price. Therefore, both businesses' Unity and Matterport should be able to influence the Metaverse.

Conclusion

The metaverse is on the way, regardless of whether people are happy with it or not. The metaverse will be the emergence of NFTs, cryptocurrency, especially when it comes to blockchain-based games, decentralized applications (dapps) and the technology of virtual or augmented reality. After Facebook's change of name to Meta in November 2021 people who were unaware of the metaverse have been taken in and the widespread acceptance of its upcoming integration into the digital world throughout the world provides crypto investors who are familiar with the metaverse technology that currently exists, a chance to make money from the technology.

Future of crypto lies in its complete integration into the metaverse and being accepted as a legitimate payment method. Like NFTs, steps are being made to dispel the myths surrounding decentralization that could dissuade some people from changing and also to end the mining process of proof-of-work in favor of other, completely renewable, green-energy proofs of blockchain technology.

Mark Zuckerberg, the CEO of Facebook will be a major player in guiding the metaverse revolution due to his massive platform and massive amount of money and his personal involvement into the venture. For the metaverse that is already established it is expected that more people be aware of the blockchain and start playing games as a play-to-earn model and frequently making use of AR and VR technologies that provide fully immersive experiences that could assist in many aspects of our lives, including healthcare and education.

The metaverse can pose some social risks such as addiction, privacy and security concerns, environmental risks in the move to renewable energy, as well as the technological challenges related to receiving funding, creating unique or immersive user experiences as well as discovering what people want to use, there's plenty of time to make it better and the support that it receives provides confidence in the hope that its risks and issues are well-managed.

Beginning with a idea of a virtual world in a book the metaverse has advanced a great distance. Certain games employ metaverse-like technology but do not call their games "metaverse," whereas others include a blend of games using blockchain that offer the player with monetary rewards for their participation as well as traditional games that make digital social connections within an AR/VR setting and have been doing so for a long time before Meta's rebirth declared them as metaverse.

When you are investing in NFTs, cryptocurrency and blockchain gaming The golden rule is to never invest more than you're at ease losing due to the extreme fluctuations of these markets that are not centralized. The aspects of investing such as diversifying your portfolio, and being aware of when to cash out are important to be aware of. Be sure to check all the information you are planning to invest or purchase to ensure that you do not fall for the scams that are prevalent in the crypto space, particularly